THE
SECRET POWER
OF THE
ROSARY

111 Daily Meditations for Peace and Healing of Families and Nations

BARBARA KLOSS

St. Dominic Media

Quotes about the power of the Rosary:

"If you say the Rosary faithfully until death, I do assure you that, in spite of the gravity of your sins you shall receive a never fading crown of glory."
-St. Louis de Montfort

"The Rosary is the most excellent form of prayer and the most efficacious means of attaining eternal life. It is the remedy for all our evils, the root of all our blessings. There is no more excellent way of praying." - Pope Leo XIII

"The Rosary is a powerful weapon to put the demons to flight and to keep oneself from sin....If you desire peace in your hearts, in your homes, and in your country, assemble each evening to recite the Rosary. Let not even one day pass without saying it, no matter how burdened you may be with many cares and labors." - Pope Pius XI

"Among all the devotions approved by the Church, none has been so favored by so many miracles as the Rosary devotion." - Pope Pius IX

The SECRET POWER of the ROSARY

Declarations

Since the abolition of Canons 1399 and 2318 of the former Code of Canon Law by Pope Paul VI in AAS 58 (1966), p. 1186, publications about new apparitions, revelations, prophecies, miracles, etc., have been allowed to be distributed and read by the faithful without the express permission of the Church, providing that they contain nothing that contravenes faith and morals. This means no imprimatur is necessary. However it is welcome!

In Chapter II, No. 12 of the Second Vatican Council's *Lumen Gentium,* we read:

"The Holy Spirit... distributes special gifts among the faithful of every rank... Such gifts of grace, whether they are of special enlightenment or whether they are spread more simply and generally, must be accepted with gratefulness and consolation, as they are specially suited to, and useful for, the needs of the Church...Judgment as to their genuineness and their correct use lies with those who lead the Church and those whose special task is not indeed to extinguish the spirit but to examine everything and keep that which is good." (confer 1 Thess. 5: 19-21)

"That private revelations occur in all times is evident as appears from the testimony of the Sacred Scripture and tradition. To stamp these testimonies as untruths gives scandal and bears witness to impiety."

Cardinal Bona

BARBARA KLOSS

The SECRET POWER of the ROSARY

INDEX

PAGES

THE
SECRET POWER
OF THE
ROSARY

**111 Daily Meditations for
Peace and Healing of
Families and Nations**

BARBARA KLOSS

INTRODUCTION

This booklet came into existence from meditations carried out on the first Saturdays of each month, and is, therefore, a response to the call of the Mother of God for devotion to her Immaculate Heart and her desire to rescue the world from moral and physical misery.

The reflections were written by a certain person in Poland during the course of a few years. We do not know her name. Neither do we know the name of her spiritual director who preserved these writings and passed them on for printing.

Acquaintance with this booklet shows distinctly that it has a charismatic character. Charisma means a supernatural grace, a gift from God, freely given and granted to some people not so much for one's own use and salvation, as for the salvation of other people. As it was in the Old Testament, and in the first century of Christianity, so also at the present time God faithfully imparts His Own Gifts for the building up and strengthening of the people of God. The Second Vatican Council confirms: "Allotting His gifts according as He wills (cf. Cor. 12:7), He also distributes special gifts among the faithful of every rank. By these gifts He makes them fit and ready to undertake various tasks and offices for the building up of the Church, as it is written 'the manifestation of the Spirit is given to everyone for profit' (1 Cor. 12:7). Whether these charisms be very remarkable or more simple and widely diffused, they are to be received with thanksgiving and consolation since they are fitting and useful for the needs of the Church. Obviously, judgement about their authenticity, and about the proper bringing into effect of them, belongs to the authorities of the Church, "who are especially called to this, not to quench the Spirit, but to test everything and to hold fast to what is good" (1. Tess. 5:12 and 19:21) (Constitution of the Church No. 12).

Moreover, this booklet in all respects is conformable with the teaching of the Church. Through a human instrument, gifted with a charisma, there speaks sometimes the Mother of God, and at other times an Angel or the Saints, and sometimes there are herein only the personal meditations of the person who wrote these "Rosary Thoughts".

Not prejudging in anything the supernatural character of these thoughts, but in everything subjecting my own judgement to the authority of the Church, Marianie Prowincji N.M.P. Matki Miłosierdzia, willingly issues this booklet in the conviction that it effects much good, and it allows worshippers of the Holy Rosary to see this prayer in a new light.

Ks. Julian Chrósciechowski M.I.C.
Provincial.

FOREWORD

I came to know Miss Barbara Kloss in Szymonowo. She was an unusually pious and an unusually suffering person. She was a person who aroused respect and admiration. She was never parted from the Rosary. Her First Saturday meditations bear the stamp of true inspiration.

- This book "Rosary Meditations" came into being from deep love of the Mother Most Holy, of whom Barbara Kloss was a faithful slave.
- This book, "Rosary Meditations", came into existence against a background of unceasing Rosaries said by Miss Barbara.
- This book "Rosary Meditations", developed from the extraordinary sufferings of Miss Barbara, and from her extraordinary piety.
- This book, "Rosary Meditations", came into existence under the inspiration of the Spirit of God.

The present times are the period of the great battle of the spirits. To the true devotees of the Mother of God the victory in this battle is guaranteed. To such worshippers, Barbara Kloss belonged. In the times when it seemed that the Rosary was out-of-date, she held it, continually, in her hands, and she prompted those around her to the continuous Rosary, and finally, she gave us this book, "Rosary Meditations", which has encouraged many to the prayer of the Rosary.

BARBARA KLOSS

Miss Barbara found The Mother of God, in entirety, in the Rosary: there she sought Her and there she found Her.

May we also, as soon as possible, find the Mother of God, victorious always, in the Rosary prayer.

Bishop ZbigniewJ.Kraszewski.

(Warsaw).

The SECRET POWER of the ROSARY

REMEMBERANCE OF BARBARA KLOSS

I came to know Barbara Kloss in the autumn of 1948. Earlier in this same year I had been sent from Dublin as an envoy of the Legion of Mary to Poland. The President of the Legion of Mary praesidium at the Cathedral in Lublin said to me: "This matter demands great prayer and great suffering; I am giving to you the address of one of the most spiritual persons in Warsaw; tell her about the Legion.

When I found Barbara in Warsaw she was living with her aged Mother at her brother's place. He was a lawyer. She was recovering from tuberculosis, and at this time she was also suffering very much from inflammation of the entire cavity of the mouth after extraction of teeth. If I remember well it was called "sepsis".

I related all about the Legion of Mary, and because the basis of the Legion is "The True Devotion to the Blessed Virgin Mary" by St. Louis Grignon de Montfort, I spoke also about this devotion. At that time it was still possible to buy this booklet in the bookshop, St. Wojciecha. I purchased it and presented it to Barbara. From that time until the end of her life she practised this devotion faithfully.

I told her also about the revelations in Fatima, and Barbara began the devotion of the Five First Saturdays. Included in this devotion is the extra promise of meditation on the Rosary for fifteen minutes in the company of the Mediatrix of all Graces – the Queen of the Holy Rosary.

From the beginning the First Saturday meditations

were dictated to Barbara. Nobody invented this dictation, and it went against all of her abilities. She heard, inwardly, a voice and wrote down according to inward dictations.

For the last five years of her life Barbara was ill with disfiguring, incurable rheumatism. She was paralysed. The meditations on the Rosary she dictated to me. On two occasions, at the time when I was busy at Jasna Góra conducting the continuous Rosaries for the Holy Father, she dictated them to her nurse.

Barbara's mystical state was surrounded with secrecy. No one knew about it, not even the nearest in the household. The near Zakopane where she was a catechist, in Kroscienk nad Dunajcem, in Idzbark (parafia Ostród) and finally in Szymonowo (woj. Olsztyn).

The edition through O.O. Marianów in London in 1971 contained 111 meditations. The Warsaw Curia published 105 meditations in 1975. In all there are 313 meditations. Many were lost, and among these were priceless and unrepeatable meditations on The Lord's Prayer.

Barbara was a young lady of very great culture. She was a Polish scholar with an ardent love of Polish literature and especially of Mickiewicz Słowacki's poem: "IN THE MIDST OF DISCORD, THE LORD STRIKES AN ENORMOUS BELL," she knew from memory and often recited it to us in those days, and at that time we did not think that this was already so near.

To my understanding Barbara Kloss was a completely exceptional person. I met her – as I have written – after her recovery to health. It seems that the Mother of God chose her simply as a tool in bringing about Her great

The SECRET POWER of the ROSARY

plan regarding the people of Poland. In sufferings, prayer and sacrifice she was burned, as a brick is burned, to be suitable for the building of a basilica which is a Divine mystery, and is called "The Mystical Body". The corner-stone and the vault of this basilica is the Pope. This also was the basis of Barbara's sufferings and desires – the Popes in general and in particular the Polish Pope.

The Mother of God, through Barbara Kloss, pre-pared us, so that we would, without hesitation, accept the Marian Movement of Priests. I had previously heard about Father Gobbi in a general way, and I knew that it is in this precise way that the Mother of God conquers and crushes the head of the serpent.

The Seat of Wisdom wished to pour out the wisdom of the Rosary on Poland, and through Poland on the whole world. First She burned the head of Barbara in the fire of suffering. This is why she was obliged to have tubercular meningitis, and then abscesses. After this, inflammation of the skin, which caused Barbara to become chapped, like the earth in a time of drought. She lost all her hair, but after-wards it grew again.

When I received a command from the Mother of God to organise the continuous Rosaries for the Holy Fa-ther it seemed easy to me. I was prepared for this when Fa-ther Stephen Gobbi told me in Częstochowa on the 6th Sep-tember, 1976 that I must gather Priests in Poland for the Marian Movement. I knew that through many years and many ways the Mother of God had prepared me for this.

Yesterday at Holy Mass with the Holy Father I glanced at the little chain of Slavery of Love on my wrist. Yes, it was precisely on this chain that the Most Holy

Mother brought me to this wonderful chapel on this wonderful day of Saint Francis Xavier. Certainly I owe everything to the Mother of God, but in an indirect way, to her instrument – Barbara Kloss.

The last words of Barbara to us after the operation on an intestine were: "I love you, (pl.) I love you with all my heart! I thank you."

I replied: "I thank you Madam for the great holy cause, the great experience, for great holy wisdom, for the great holy action."

Her last words to her nurse were: "Take off this chain and give it to Anatol."

On this chain of the Slavery of Love according to St. Louis Marie de Montfort, the Holy Angels brought me, at the command of the Queen, to the Chapel of the Holy Father.

"To the Victor I will give a new name and a little white stone." If I were to be asked what new name to give Barbara, without hesitation I would cry out: "THE POWER OF LOVE".

Barbara Kloss died on the 15th January, 1981 in the hospital in Morąg and was buried in the cemetery in Miłomłyn.

Five years ago Barbara requested me to go to Warsaw and to ask Ks. Bishop Z. J. Kraszewski to come to Szymonowo, because she, being paralysed was not able to go to him. To my joyful surprise Ks. Bishop set out immediately, and she revealed her secret to him. From that time Ks. Bishop visited her each year in Szymonowo, and administered to her the Sacraments of Penance and the Eucharist.

The SECRET POWER of the ROSARY

I believe that Barbara Kloss is before the throne of the Queen of the Rosary, with powerful love for the Fatherland and with especial love for the Holy Father; that she is with Sr. Faustina – especially beloved; that she and St. Philomena and Blessed Catherine Tekawitha are with the triumphant Poles in Heaven

For thirty years I lived under the same roof as Barbara Kloss. I affirm that during all this time I have never perceived in her any of the thousands of silly weaknesses, nor any of the thousands of unwise ways, such as we have.

I finish with invocations dictated through Barbara Kloss: "All countrymen, who in the state of grace, shed blood for the Faith and Fatherland in the struggle with heathens and enemies of the Cross, pray for us.

"All countrymen and countrywomen now in the glory of Heaven who with prayers, tears, work, suffering and sacrifice desire to obtain by their entreaties the Kingdom of God for the Fatherland and for the whole world, pray for us; pray for the Holy Father!"

And because to day is the First Friday I will include one more of our daily prayers:

"Most Sacred Heart of Jesus, enclose in the protection of Your Divine Heart our Holy Father John Paul II. Be his Light, his Strength, and his Consolation! Amen."

(Signed) Anatol Kaszczuk,
Szymonowo.

TABLE OF CONTENTS for Volume I:

20. It is necessary to live the Rosary.
21. This weapon will defeat our enemies, and this weapon will ascertain our safety.
22. Unity with the Most Holy Trinity – this is called happiness.
23. Mother of Mercy.
24. From the Rosary there arises a tower of defense.
25. It is necessary for people to conceive that on which an offering depends.
26. The Rosary – the Old Testament.
27. Do not be troubled.
28. The Lord Jesus sleeping amid the storm.
29. My beloved ones are to be with the Heart of the Mother Most Holy, and with the Heart of Her Divine Son.
30. Devotion to the Most Sacred Heart of the Lord Jesus and the Rosary.
31. Martha, you are anxious about many things; only one is necessary.
32. The Rosary is the most direct, the easiest and most important way to unity with the Lord Jesus through Mary.
33. "No one says the Rosary – only in the Holy Spirit."
34. The Rosary said well and lived through.
35. The Rosary must have its due place.
36. The authority of the Immaculate Heart of Mary, before which all Heaven bows in humility.
37. Let us thank the Lord for the graces bestowed on the Immaculate Heart of the Mother of God, and let us give thanks for the graces bestowed on St. Elizabeth at the Visitation.

3 8. The Rosary will soon be the indispensable line of rescue. XIV.

3 9. Advent, Advent, Advent.

4 0. He one who is not armed with the Rosary, supported by the Rosary, strengthened by the Rosary, and purified by the Rosary need not think of coming forward to fight with satan. And who is?

4 1. The Holy Spirit looks for someone on whom He may repose.

4 2. Let the Queen of the Universe be greeted, "Full of Grace"

4 3. I came to start a fire on earth and how I wish that it was blazing.

4 4. The rhythm of saying the Rosary.

4 5. I live, no longer I, there live in me the mysteries of the Rosary of Jesus and Mary.

4 6. From the moment one knows that this is from God, it must be absolutely accepted.

4 7. The Kingdom of Mary is in you.

4 8. The Rosary and the world – the Joyful Mysteries.

4 9. Twelve statements about the Rosary – this is as a Creed.

5 0. The spirit of penance (Joyful part).

5 1. The sowing of the Rosary.

5 2. This means that one would flow into the harbour of salvation quickly, without any deviation.

5 3. And through the joining of the voice of your heart with the voice of the Immaculate Heart of Mary, it takes on the value of horrifying hell and enrapturing Heaven.

5 4. And they saw no one, only the same Jesus.

55. In each mystery there is compassionate love and mercy for you – we are celebrating true devotion to the Divine Mercy.
56. The one who hopes in me will not be shamed.
57. Oh that you would know what happens when, at your request, the Mother of God intercedes for you.
58. Look, My daughter, on this Maternal Heart.
59. The Rosary struggles with hell.
60. The Heart of the Divine Mother is easy to find, to know and to imitate.
61. The Rosary before the Blessed Sacrament has an inconceivable power of intercession.
62. Absolute ceasing of self-seeking.
63. With the Rosary in the hand and on the lips, with a humble and trusting heart, you can expect beyond measure, more than your poor tiny heads and hearts can conceive and feel.
64. The Rosary is the twofold gift of love.
65. The adoration of the Most Holy Face.
66. The Rosary is a great, holy act. Through faith in the power of the Rosary one receives its power.
67. In each mystery there is a struggle. This is a direct struggle with satan.
68. Fatima is the turning point in the history of mankind. The Joyful part – of the choice of Heaven.
69. And therefore, in these things there is nothing trifling, which it would be possible to disregard, and there is nothing, which if disregarded, would not be enormous in its consequences.
70. There are lonely Queens, the widowed and those who have awaited exile.

71. Jesus died – X. I am the Mother of the resurrected Christ.
72. My Son, behold the world, which You gave me, purified and prepared by Me! Reign!
73. XII mystery, the Ascension. Either I win Heaven or I lose it.
74. Let such a family say to itself: "We wish to be such a Bethany".
75. A word about the bringing forth of the Church in the thirteenth mystery.
76. Jesus living in Mary and Jesus living in us. This leads us quickly to the age of Christ.
77. The saying of the Rosary teaches us devotion to the Will of God.
78. The characteristic of the action of the Holy Spirit is urgency, and the result – everything changes.
79. The most perfect creature, which came from the Hands of God, is the Mother of God.
80. All devotion to the Mother of Sorrows is included in the Rosary.
81. Heart of Mary most closely united with the Heart of Jesus, pray for us.
82. Harmony with the Will of God.
83. This we say to you: Unceasing Hail Marys flowing from your hearts and your lips unite Us with you and are a condition of the victory.
84. The Ascension and the Assumption; these are the present signposts.
85. And in this everything has to be love, which is the sole payment for the Love of My Heart.

The SECRET POWER of the ROSARY

86. Where the Rosary is – where the Rosary truly is – there also is persecution and victory. Mediation between God and us.
87. All the first part of the Rosary is full of St. Joseph.
88. I am the Queen – Queen of Heaven, Queen of the Universe, Queen of Poland.
89. Christo confixus sum cruci. I live, not I, Christ lives in me.
90. Omnipotenta Orans. Then it has to have this, which is necessary – this is oratio omnipotens. The almighty intercessory prayer with Almighty Force.
91. There must be a unity between the interior of a person, the given mystery and its Angel.
92. The joy of both Most Holy Hearts from the fulfilment of the Redemption.
93. The joy of the Kingdom of the Heart of Mary is preparation of the most beautiful crowns for her children.
94. Suiting the mystery to life and life to the mystery.
95. Before I put these souls as flowers before the Divine Throne, I will first come, at death, with all the graces for salvation.
96. The criterion in many matters, as they are, from which they originated and to which goal they are striving.
97. Share the Rosary with others, because one does not become poor through this, but becomes rich.
98. The Rosary is the criterion of holiness.
99. The Glorious part – introduction.
100. Devotion to God the Father in the Rosary, and three means of meditation.

101. The Holy Angels and the Rosary. May God be adored in His Angels and in His Saints.
102. The Rosary prepares for the hour of death.
103. Mary conceived without sin. The Most Holy names of Jesus and Mary
104. The way of the deathbed of the Lord Jesus.
105. "Wine which the Virgin bears … Bread of the strong."
106. Take off your shoes, because the place where you are standing is holy.
107. Such is the school of life, the school of death, the school of triumph!
108. The Rosary is the guide to holiness.
109. The Visitation.
110. Temperance and work.
111. The heart is as the feelings within it.

End.

MOTTO:

"Jesus desires that I would be more known and more loved."
(From the revelations at Fatima)

"I am entirely in the Rosary; seek me there – find me there."

The SECRET POWER of the ROSARY

1. The Rosary has to be the joy of your hearts, the light of your minds, the desire of your wills, the fire uniting you and welding you with Heaven. It has to be the unfathomable mine of treasures, which are hidden and which I am giving you through my Immaculate hands. From you there is only required: the will to accept it and to pray it, the time sacrificed, a humble and pious disposition, and a bit of effort in concentration and prayer. Do not begrudge this, nor push it aside so that somehow, room has to be made for it in the last quarter-hour of the day.

The remainder, that is to say everything else, is the action of the Holy Spirit, which gives knowledge of the Saviour and His mysteries, and gives love to the Father, which has the effect of causing souls, who are burning with this ember of love of God, to become open to comprehension and to the plunging of themselves into the love of God. Then the words of the Son of God are realised: *"THE KINGDOM IS IN YOU. THE EVERLASTING AND UNIVERSAL KINGDOM, THE KINGDOM OF TRUTH AND LIFE, THE KINGDOM OF HOLINESS AND GRACE, THE KINGDOM OF JUSTICE, LOVE AND PEACE."* (Preface of the feast of Christ the King).

2. The Rosary is the inexhaustible treasure of the countless graces of God in the One Holy Trinity, but in order to profit from the Rosary it is necessary to have faith, which quickly changes into the joy of experience.

The Rosary is mine and demands humility, because it gives what I desire, and not what you will and what you desire.

The Rosary is yours. It is given to you for always. You have it for every moment and for every need. Its utilisation and effect depends on you. It demands faithfulness and perseverance.

The Rosary is for all who are winning our Hearts, my Son's and mine. It unites everyone living on earth that revere and love it, and those who are already in triumph, with the combined strength of victory.

3. The Rosary is the gift which was bought with the Blood of my Son. If such is its origin and such is its seal, let nothing surprise you regarding opposition to its recognition, acceptance, and extension, because the devil, the world and the flesh, in common, fight against it. ***Put me as a seal on your heart.*** This means that each one would have his own beloved mystery for a certain period and. after saying the Rosary, would satiate himself with it, because it alone explains, simplifies and deepens many things in the soul. With the Rosary it is easy to knock on the gate of the Mercy of God.

4. Jesus desires that I would be more known and loved. And I desire that the Heart of My Triumphant Son would everywhere reign: in you and here with you. Both of us desire your happiness and your good for the glory of Our Heavenly Father. These desires of both our Sacred Hearts bring about the outpouring of mercy, and it is necessary to see mercy, to give thanks for it and to implore it for yourselves and for the whole world. The Rosary is for the accomplishment of this, because in it one repeats ***"Blessed art thou among women, and blessed is the fruit of thy womb, Jesus."*** These words are so very important because they establish the beginning of this adoration which has to be carried over to eternity. It is necessary to speak them with great love and humility, in the happiness that already here on earth you are permitted to pronounce them, because they are the beginning of what will endure through all eternity – the adoration of mercy. ***Misericordias Domini in aeternum cantabo.*** In the fifteen mysteries we adore Mercy.

May the most wonderful action in the most wonderful causes of the most wonderful Mother be adored!

May the Mercy of God in the most wonderful privileges of the most wonderful power of the Lord Most Wonderful, be adored!

May the most wonderful action in the wonderful ways which lead, by wonderful means, most wonderful vocations, be praised!

5. Each victory over evil hastens the arrival and is my victory, because I received all of them first from my Son.

Each victory over evil hastens the arrival of my kingdom.

The condition of these victories is the faithful saying of the Rosary.

I am wholly in the Rosary; seek me there. I am wholly in the Rosary; find me there.

6. I am truth. All my words are justice and truth, just as my Son said about Himself, that He is Truth.

The Rosary is truth, and proclaims the truth. Whoever loves the Rosary loves the truth, and, through saying it piously, finds the truth. Truth will be in his thoughts, knowledge and judgement. In me, and through me, – through me with the given means which is the Rosary – this truth comes, and fulfils these words*: Qui in me operantur non peccabunt.* (They who work in me do not sin). And the words that I am the shortest way to the Truth, to the Son, and to God, come true.

The Rosary gives this. The Rosary is this; and therefore I call and beg so much for the Rosary, and for that reason it is so combated – just the Rosary.

7. The world is swamped in errors. The Rosary is truth, proclaims truth and combats for the truth. Through the saying of the Rosary truth penetrates into the soul, because with the saying of it the mind and heart acts; the mind meditates, and the heart radiates itself, keeping itself near to the Mother and Son, as well as to their Friends who are in each mystery, and who are taking part in each mystery, and so the soul satiates itself with truth, and absorbs it, so that it can flow over into other souls. Without the Rosary, not only is there an absence of this, but there is also a deficiency of the barrier, which protects from deviation into wrong ways. This explains to you the state of the world.

Each mystery meditated upon as a separate whole has its own power and purpose, but all fifteen together is an army called to battle array under my rein. Let whoever prays the Rosary remember and know that praying the Rosary well does more than if he had built a great edifice or had worked on inventions inspiring enchantment! Often satan acts there, but know that whoever finds me finds life and salvation from the Lord, and remember that I am entirely in the Rosary; there seek me; there find me. This is a reminder and an encouragement, which has to impel to a greater zeal in the praying of the Rosary. There has to be more Rosaries and they have to be better, in order to spread open the floodgates of the graces of my Immaculate Heart of Gold, soon to be triumphant......Amen.

8.　　　I am near. I am near to all who call on me in spirit and in truth. Look for me on the ways of the Saviour, and it is precisely in the Rosary that you do this. ***He who finds me finds life and attains salvation from the Lord.***

It is necessary that the world would know what the Rosary is:

It is the search for my Son and me.

It is an endeavour, with the ultimate purpose of saving souls, through the sanctification of life by means of the Rosary.

It is the weapon for the struggle, and the consolation in repose.

It is the condition of victory.

It is the spring, which does not dry up – the inexhaustible source of grace.

It is my will, my desire, and my demand!

It is my gift – the gift from, the Mother of God and your Mother – for the poor, and for the children who remain in terrible danger.

It is the visible sign of the protection and seal of the chosen.

It is the joy of the Angels and the happiness of the Saints.

It is the horror and the terror of the devils that, through it, are defeated.

It is the most direct, the shortest and the most certain link of Heaven with earth.

It is the treasure of the poor and the power of the valiant.

Lastly, it is the joy of a child having fulfilled an obligation with love, and the hope of reward both here and hereafter.

This absorption of love, drop by drop, from the fifteen mysteries of the redemption is like the refreshing rain needed for the yielding of good fruit from good earth.

9.   My Immaculate Heart receives everything and waits.

THE ROSARY: The first sign – is respect for it.
Respect for the Rosary results in faith in the Rosary – faith in its power – and it also results in love for the Rosary. If this is so, which means if this, my gift, is in you and you are offering it to Me, then in this way My Heart is already consoled. It is always consoled as long as I find it in your hearts, and I am receiving respect, faith, hope and love.

The SECRET POWER of the ROSARY

Therefore, those who hate me hate my Rosary. Unfortunates!

So often, pitying, I have come to earth with love and the gift of my mercy, and always with a reminder about the Rosary. Trust!

The time has come for my Rosary. It is your weapon!

I have told you before that I am wholly in the Rosary. Seek me there and find me there. "I am with you. Let not your hearts be troubled, nor afraid," said My Son. Believe in Him, although in the boat He slept! Love each mystery.

Now, in conclusion, embracing in thought all fifteen mysteries, keep on to the end, in order to know the trail of my royal ways, because I am leading you after me. Amen

10. It is said about the Lord Jesus, that He did all things well. We believe that it is possible to say the same about His Mother, and we have, in the Rosary, the way in which the Lord Jesus and His Most Holy Mother do all things well. Every person, when he concentrates on his own life and investigates into it, can find his life again in each mystery. For example the Lord Jesus credits goodness only to God, but we ourselves desire it. We have to strive to be controlled by it, and most of all to embrace it. The Rosary has the priceless worth of recalling to mind the deficiencies in oneself, as well as the likeness required to imitate the Lord Jesus and His Most Holy Mother. This inner study, *Noverim me – Noverim Te* (May I know myself – May I know You) teaches this work and simplifies it.

Undoubtedly not always, not every time, does the saying of the Rosary reveal this twofold abyss – the misery of the people and the mercy of God – but finally the time comes when this, as it were, unconsciously happens. Therefore, in Rosary meditation it is good to make such a comparison to oneself, and to people: – God-Made-Man acts like His Mother, so God-Made-Man suffers like His Mother, and so, I? What is my place in this mystery, and what is its place in my life?

11.   (I still do not believe, as I ought, in the power of the Rosary).

Ask, through the Rosary, for faith in the Rosary, and in its action. The Rosary in the hands of the saints was always the same – although long ago it was shorter – but they were different, and because they said it with all their souls, so zealously, and with such humility and thanksgiving, it was permitted to them to say this Marian Psalter. Thus they united with the angels of the mystery, and were under their influence and, so tenderly, united in the great powerful army fighting, for the cause of Heaven against hell, for souls. Thus they were faithful in their service; thus they were living with the Rosary, and the time devoted to the Rosary was first and most important. First, that is, in the knowledge of the importance of prayer, and not on the other hand, of the time they were giving. So they moved every bead with love, confident of finding it in eternity. In this way they looked with reverence on the greatness and importance of the Rosary, as my gift, so that for them it effected my promises, and the words of my Son about moving a mountain with faith, and miracles were so universal that with some it was possible for them to become common. Then there were those who lost the simple heart, which rational satan confused. He turned their will round towards himself, and knowledge and judgement he warped, and my Rosary, which was the first and most important barrier against error, those unfortunate heretics threw out, and they became enemies.

The Rosary has to return to its primary importance and quality, and through the Rosary the unity of the nations has to be brought about, in the unity of holy faith. This has to come about before the fulfilment of the world. This is told to you today, for you and for everybody.   Amen.

12.   It is necessary to go beyond limits when trusting in the power of the Rosary. It is necessary to think about the Rosary, never as a burden but always as a gift of love. The Rosary never weighs down whoever knows all this, but rather it gives him wings.

The Presentation, (2nd February), is a great feast of the Rosary. The majority of people do not think about this feast. The joy of the mystery of the Presentation is seasoned with the bitter foreboding of the sorrowful mysteries, and yet the joy of this mystery and the one that follows it is full and perfect, because whether it announces the piercing of the Heart with the sword of sorrow, or the pain from the moment of losing the Child Jesus, that joy which is contained in part two of these mysteries is already in effect, because the joy of the Redemption is already present and acting, and because all this is the way to the third part of the Rosary, the glorious mysteries, and to the final goals contained in them, which are the highest gifts of the Most Holy Trinity for the Mother Most Holy, and for each soul united with Her. So it is with everything in life, and it is necessary to look at everything, to accept it, and to live through it in this way. This is the advice and teaching of The Blessed Lady, which is that for which you are coming to her so that your joy may be full and that no one can take it from you. Amen.

13.   I am always wishing to speak to you whenever you wish to speak to me, and I am also wishing to speak to you at times when you do not wish to speak to me. Above all I desire and like to speak, and I am speaking, through the Rosary, with the Rosary, and in the Rosary. I am speaking to you there about my own life, and the giving of self to the Most High God, about joys and suffering, about prayer and work, about unity with God through love, and the unity of my own will with His Most Holy Will, about the feelings of my Heart; the Heart of the Mother Most Sorrowful, and yet always in the same deep essence of the greatest happiness. This happiness flowed from the possession of Jesus, and all was for the greatest glory of God.

I am speaking to you, and showing that in the Rosary all this is easy; that this way is the sure, infallible, and only way which is intended for each one, and it is approached through me and by me, as you say, it was trodden. Its tracks are strong and distinct, and I, when I appear on it, am going beside you and with you. Why then do you worry and fear? Because if a person only brings himself to a loving act of good will, I will, for this initial effort, be doing this way with each one. This you have to know and remember! Enter often into the feelings of my Heart. And now it is permitted to go over every mystery in thought, from my joyful FIAT, through the most sorrowful FIAT to the most humble in the glorious mysteries of which the crown is my unending Magnificat. This is my testament for you! This is a living testament, because I am living and present in these mysteries, and I am looking at how you are receiving this, how you are proceeding, and to what extent I am present in each child of my inheritance.

14.   *"In meditation my Heart was inflamed."*

Today is the first Saturday, and again, all over the earth, my children are gathering. I have many of them, and this is the joy of my Immaculate Heart. I have many who only offer to me the first Saturdays and many others who do not wish to make this offering, and then there are those who were giving me this but no longer wish to do so.

It is said about the Lord Jesus that He did all things well, and it is the same with His Mother. If, therefore, one wishes to do one's best, one should imitate the Son of God and His Mother.

It was said in the meditation at the beginning, that it is necessary for each one to meditate about himself, in the Rosary, thus:

What can I take from the given mystery to apply to my own life? How can I unite with Mary and her Divine Son in this mystery?

In what way have I to discern what is necessary for me in the given mystery, so that the fruits would be good, so that everything would be done well?

In order to do away with the existence of the Rosary, so that people would be deprived of the Rosary, the devil has made heresies. Each mystery of the Rosary strikes at heresy.

15. Whoever calls to me – I am with him. A call to me is never in vain, but when I come – I come always with an abundance of graces and the great love of my maternal Heart. I desire to be called upon. I desire to bestow grace. My Heart is overfilled with love, and therefore, I bring the Rosary, I ask for the Rosary, and I urge that it be said well. The whole thing is this – that it would be said with unflinching strength and a lively faith, so that in each mystery faith would be strengthened and enlivened, and so that exactly what the Mother of God said and what she wishes would, in each mystery, be strengthened and confirmed in us, until there is such a Rosary that will crumble rocks, and will work miracles easily.

16. *De Maria numquam satis*. (About Mary there is never enough)

In regard to the Rosary it is necessary to say (because it is exactly so) that the more you know it – the more you love it, and the more you love it – the more you know it. Its power is immense, its action manifold, its domain unending, but the vast majority of people, even those who

The SECRET POWER of the ROSARY

love it and say it, do not know its chief and essential meaning, which is the disablement of the demons. It is necessary by means of the Rosary to expose this mystery of all their activity in everything. Hence, particularly and universally, is known its efficacious action in the healing of the sick, in consoling the sorrowful, in helping the afflicted, in rescue and defence in times of danger, in the subduing of evil, in the return of sinners, in bringing about a happy death, in the sanctification of hearts, in the purifying of thoughts, in a word – in drawing near to God Himself, through all kinds of obstacles, which are being erected by all those, who from the first moment of the rebellion up until now, have persevered in this, and who will continue to persevere in this forever, because this is what they wish. Therefore, it is not permitted to remove the Rosary. Many people think that it is useful, pleasant, efficacious, and so on, but they must believe that such a gift of the Mother of God is above all her devotions, and they have to know, that it is indispensable. It is necessary to pray about this, that this truth will penetrate into life.

17. I am the Queen of the Rosary. The Rosary is my kingdom, my inheritance. The Rosary is victorious, because such is the most Holy Will of God that it would be an inducement to the carrying of the victory. The world is in darkness! The world is in error! The world is in persistent calamities, but let you trust. My beloved son Leo (Leo XIII) wrote that the dragon is pouring out filth. The Rosary is the barrier, the obstacle against the fires of hell. Through the Rosary islands are created, where evil spirits are not allowed to operate. How would it be with you, and how would it be with all of you, if you had not got your Rosaries? Hell has plans.

18.   I know that to day I have to take the mystery of the Ascension and the mystery of the Assumption, in order to base everything on the promise that the sufferings of this time are not worthy of the coming glory, which is to be revealed. The Lord God never was, never will be, only IS.

We are living here in this changing time, which exists so that in this time here on earth proof is accomplished. It depends on the choice of good or of evil, which is made by every person, and all of this establishes the life, which we are seeing. Everyone from birth to death has the power of choice of location between two boundaries. It follows from this that not only do we have to stay in this variability, but also we have to draw near to God Who is, and Who endures.

In Him is peace and in Him is the fullness of all that we need, so that these changing times do not carry us off. This is not neutralisation, nor nirvana, nor as with others, a dissolving into all that exists. It is the acceptance of the gift of Redemption – *"My peace I leave with you, My peace I give to you, not as the world gives am I giving to you".* Let you persevere in peace now. This means to persevere in peace amid change. The acceptance of this peace is obedience.

The saints settled everything is peace and in their action there was the power of God. In order to persevere in peace, without regard to what is happening around us, we have the assistance of the Rosary, but above all the XII and XIV mysteries. [The Ascension and the Assumption]. The Rosary gives everything; it arranges, points, and leads, and therefore, it is so very necessary.

19. The Lord Jesus taught the apostles how to pray. At their request He gave them a prayer. The Mother of God also gave a prayer. For us, it is only necessary to believe, to accept, to fulfil and offer it. The Mother Most Holy possesses simple, obedient, faithful and chaste souls, because it is only such that can fulfil Her desires. This chastity of soul is a necessary condition for comprehension of the Rosary; the comprehension of the sense of mystery. It is called a mystery because for one it is uncovered, and for another it is closed. The Rosary is an immediate gauge of souls. The power of the Rosary lies in the praying of it constantly, daily. This constancy and continuous praying of it gives, at the end of life, a similar result as a stream does, a little stream, whose waters cross over into the great river and falls into the sea.

20. It is necessary to live the Rosary and to skilfully entwine it into one's own life, in each situation. Dissenters are not acquainted with the Rosary; they know nothing, or almost nothing, about it. Despite this they hate it, fight it, ridicule it and deride it, because they sense the power hidden in it.

The Mother of God did not abandon her own Son. During all the time of the Way of the Cross she was a

Mother to Him. The Mother Most Holy, on the Way of the Cross, is united most closely with the Lord Jesus, and therefore, the Mother of God is also there with he children where they are suffering. The Mother Most Holy will accompany us on the way of the cross; and in everything we have to love the Will of God, just as she managed to do this. We have to have peace, we have to have trust, and do our task.

The Heart of the Mother of God accepts our sympathy with thanksgiving as if relief had actually been effected to her.

21. It is necessary to shelter under the power of the mysteries of the Rosary. It is necessary to know about this, to think about it, and to hold on to it, because when it will seem that rescue is not to be had anywhere, it is precisely from the Rosary, and through the Rosary that help will flow. From nothing else will flow strength and power and peace and safety and light. An army in battle array – is many identical soldiers. The Rosary is the same kind of army, because it is composed of many identical prayers. This weapon will paralyse our enemies, and this weapon will secure safety for us. It follows that to day we are still encouraged to look on it as an advantage to our side, because a well-said Rosary, whether by a child or an adult, with faith and piety, can become, and becomes the work of David and the defense tower, and at the same time dispatches in fear, and takes, away, the enemy's spirit. It is necessary to call to the people and to waken them from inactivity and insensibility to guard the Rosary.

The SECRET POWER of the ROSARY

Obviously, it is not possible to compare it with the Holy Mass or Holy Communion. It has, however, extraordinary power. Therefore, our work, occupations, and important obligations ought not easily to exempt us from the daily Rosary.

22. The Mother Most Holy says: "My Son said '*Well done, faithful servant'*....My mouth also repeats 'Well done, faithful servant'. This is the promise for the faithful, for the praying of the Rosary. I am the fullness of prayer. I passed all my life on earth continuously praying, and the Lord gave me the grace, so that my prayers were pleasing to Him, but through my own faithful co-operation, through my effort, they became more and more pleasing to Him – until, in the end they became most pleasing. At present my life, which is completely enclosed in the Lord is a continuous great prayer, and, according to the Will of God the Father, according to the Inspirations of the God the Spirit, and according to the Desires of God the Son, mine is the distribution of this gift, and my promise for fidelity to the Rosary is fulfilled through ever more deep and splendid prayer, through its ascending ever more higher in its degree, until it is in the most perfect union with God in the Holy Trinity, through the humanity of my Son. This union, which is foretold, is the guarantee and the gateway to everlasting union. This is called happiness.

23. In the Litany there is the invocation: "Mother of Mercy". This title and this activity is the gift of the mercy of the Most Holy Trinity. I am the Mother of Mercy, because my Son is the King of Mercy through the power of His own merit. My action, my share in the acts of my Son the Redeemer of the world, flows from the mercy with which the Holy Spirit filled my Heart. My Gifts – revelations, the Scapular, the Rosary, the Medal – is this same mercy. When disdain, reluctance and hostility towards it strikes pain in my Heart, it also strikes pain the Heart of My Son, and in the Being of the Most Holy Trinity, Whose Mercy is inexpressible, inconceivable and unlimited. But this occurs, not with the hostile, not with the atheists, not with the unbelievers, but in the Church alone, even sometimes in the same superior authority of the Church.

Oh how very necessary it is to sanctify the first Fridays and Saturdays with deep feeling and piety, in order to make recompense to Our Hearts, and to suppress the anger of the Lord.

Every sin is an act of contempt and rejection of the Mercy of God, but now people are openly showing contempt, and are transgressing plainly against the greatest Divine attribute, which is Mercy. It is necessary to pray about this, so that the world would recognise and glorify the Mercy of God, so that it would desire it, would trust in it, would be thankful for it, would be prepared in humility and faith for its reception, and that it would do all of this through my Rosary, through my hands, through my heart overflowing with mercy, because this is what pleases God the Father, God the Son and God the Holy Ghost in the most holy Will of the Most Holy Trinity, and this Will, is that same Mercy. Amen.

The SECRET POWER of the ROSARY

24. *"Let not your hearts be troubled; do not fear; Believe in the Father; believe also in Me."* Peace is the gift of Heaven. The Lord Jesus gave us His Own Mother, and she gave us the Rosary, in order to prove openly, that the same Lord Jesus is loyal to His promises: *"My peace I give you."*

From the Rosary there arises such a defense tower and such a protective wall that, irrespective of what may strike you, you should endure in peace, and make around yourselves an impregnable fortress of Rosaries. And believe that this is so.

The call for the help, defense and power of the given mystery establishes the most real efficacious protection and help, and also liberates to action the Holy Angels, whose protection and help all of you need so much, and which, in the future, you will need even more. If only people knew this, and if only they would believe this, and if only they accepted this – how many continuous Rosaries would be carried to the Queen of Angels? For satan makes, and will be making more and more greater efforts in order to dissipate this peace.

Let you persist in peace. Amen.

25. *"Let not your hearts be troubled; do not fear. Believe in the Father; believe also in Me."*

Believe in the power of the Holy Rosary. In every mystery the merits of my Son, with which I am uniting you, have sufficient overabundant power to stand as your protection, even though it would be against all hell, and against everything evil which threatens souls and bodies. It is necessary that people would comprehend that on which their offering, through my Immaculate Heart to the Eternal Father depends, and that they would do this in every mystery. Once this is grasped, everyone is able to accept and do it, everyone can, but for this faith is needed. This faith will grow, enliven, strengthen, and will work miracles. The Holy Spirit, in the measure of the depth of your humility and in the measure of your effort to seek and find me in every mystery, will come into you, enkindle in you the fire of love, unite you with Christ and bestow on you His gifts and fruits, until you are formed in Christ.

So it is necessary to present it simply and clearly to people and they will accept it. One person will rejoice with its simplicity and ease, others with its wealth and depth, and all will feel an inward impact that they did not expect, and the outward result that they requested.

26. It is not possible to reject the Old Testament and confine oneself only to the New. The piety of the Mother Most Holy blossomed forth from the Old Testament. There were the psalms and hymns. The hymn Magnificat determines the summit of these hymns. In the Old Testament the people had everything, in order to accept the Saviour, and after this they still had St. John who pointed to Him with the finger: "This is He", and still so few of the Jews, among those who knew everything about the coming Saviour, accepted Him. Those who followed Him knew only a little. They were not students of Scripture, but they were humble, and had respect for their own scholars. In the simplicity of seeing the miracles and hearing the teaching, they trusted completely. In the Old Testament God is adored directly, addressing to Him: *All things of the Lord Bless the Lord, glorify and extol Him forever. Angels of the Lord bless the Lord. Heavens of the Lord bless the Lord* ....and so on, (the song of *the three* young men. Daniel), and this is repeated many times. There were many such primeval spiritual venerations, which repeated these praises in prayer many times, and nobody was surprised at this, and even now no one is surprised when these prayers are united to the liturgical prayers: *"Bless the Lord, O My soul, and all my being bless His Holy Name."* (Ps. 102). In the Rosary it is the same, only I am united in this: *"Blessed art Thou among women and blessed is the Fruit of Thy Womb"* – and this disgusts and bores them, and the uniformity fills them with indignation – apparently – and the time spent is too long. Their thoughtlessness and callousness causes these words to become thoughtlessly and soullessly repeated. In the Old Testament it is written that those who act through Me – do not err, and for them this ought to be sufficient foundation for the constitution of a full and perfect devotion, such as God requires from His creatures. In this command of the Old Testament is the full justification, and the complete reason for the perfect devotion which is going to give the greatest glory to The Most High God in the Heavens from His creatures; and everything in me and through me, through the power of the first mystery of the Rosary, in which all others are contained, because I said: "Behold the handmaid."

There are those who do not want my service to the Lord and to you; the service whose seal is Rosary chains.

Hell roars, and orders its own: "Assail it!" And I, again, am throwing it as lines of rescue, and I await the one who grasps it. Grasp it! Grasp it, because blessed are those who in the morning, everyday, are waiting at my door. The Rosary has to be prayed daily.

" *Now then, Sons, listen to me: Blessed are those who guard my ways. Listen to the instruction, be wise and do not reject it".* (Sermon from Holy Mass, 8th December).

27. *"In Me is all hope, life and virtue ... He who finds me finds life and the outpouring of salvation from the Lord".* Believe that I am entirely in the Rosary. There you have to seek me, and there to find me, and then you find the promises of the Sacred Words of Holy Scripture concerning the Rosary. I am speaking to you to remind you about the Rosary, to remind you to strengthen your faith in its efficacy, power and consolation – your hope, life and virtue.

"Let not your hearts be troubled; fear not." - *"He who acts through Me does not err."* Many promises refer to the Rosary with the guaranty of my Son and His Deputies, and with the promises of the Holy Spirit. Holy Scripture, with my encouragement and teaching ought to gladden, strengthen and fill your hearts with peace. With the mysteries of the Rosary in your thoughts, with your hearts burning with love for them, with their holy words in your ears – let you not be troubled. With these words I am ending, and with these words – let you live: "Let you not be troubled."

The SECRET POWER of the ROSARY

28. *"Let not your hearts be troubled; do not fear"*. These are the words of the Lord Jesus, about which the Mother Most Holy reminds you, and which she passes on to us now, so that we will have power in mind and in heart to present to ourselves in the Holy Gospel the picture of the Lord Jesus sleeping amid the storm on the sea, when the alarmed apostles ran to Him with reproaches because He is sleeping – and here we are drowning. Likewise, the saying of the Rosary with faith in its power, with trust, with the assurance of the Mother Most Holy and the feeling of fulfilment of the commands of the Will of God, permits us to persevere and endure. Then in the Rosary haymaking, the measure in which this has been accepted in us and in our neighbour is proven.

29. The first Saturday meditations which the Mother of God asked of the people (through Lucy of Fatima), and for which she waits, are establishing the proof and are a sign of the truth of the words of the Holy Spirit in Scripture: *"And My Beloved to be with the sons of men"*. But the Lord Jesus desires, announces and claims, in a way most sweet, most loving, and most powerful, that each human child would desire this, would live this, and would truly be able to say: *"My love – our love is to be with the Heart of the Mother Most Holy and with the Heart of her Divine Son"*. And this is the Rosary.

30. If, in the month of June and in general, somebody wishes to constantly adore the Most Sacred Heart of the

Lord Jesus, let him do so by means of the Rosary, because every mystery of the Holy Rosary is full of the love of the Immaculate Heart of Mary for her Divine Son. Each mystery is filled with the love of the Immaculate Heart of Mary, in which is contained adoration, and worship, and thanksgiving and everything, through her perfect knowledge of this Most Sacred Heart (which nobody knows as Mary knows) and everything from the most perfect submission and unity with this Divinity, which is the abode of the Most Sacred Heart. While we, meditating on this, and wondering, and humbly desiring to imitate it, have to completely strip our hearts of even the finest dust of everything, which could not possibly be contained in both Sacred Hearts. Thus, in the rapture of love, one finds, in the easiest way, the dying away of the seed, and the goal and the way is – the Rosary, and the reason is – the love of God, and the Mother holding the hand on this road is – Mary. (When one does this one is under the action of the Holy Spirit Who gives knowledge of the Lord Jesus. As Saint Louis Grignon de Montfort says, "The Holy Spirit acts only there, where Mary is").

31.   Vision: I see a crib in which there is nothing except a manger, and the child is not in the manger, but taken out from it and laid crosswise in front of the manger, as if it were sick and abandoned. It is moving a little. There is nobody beside it. This is not the Lord Jesus. It is, as it were, a symbol of something. Such a painful impression; it is probably the heresies against the Mother of God, which wish to see the Lord Jesus without a Mother, the Church without a Mother, and us without a Mother. And there are neither Angels there, nor St. Joseph – although it is a symbol of the birth of the Lord Jesus.

And now, point by point, thoughts about the Birth of God: Where was this? Far from people; far from people God was born. There was such fuss and movement in all Bethlehem – with passionate infatuations – until it resounded. Of the Most Holy Mother, under the protection of Saint Joseph, and far from people – there God was born. The Lord Jesus is born in the souls of people, and here also there must be these same conditions of silence and removal, and everything as it was in actuality, with the presence of the Mother of God, Saint Joseph, the Angels, the Saints already on the road to the Lord Jesus, and the Mighty Magi. And in the world? Tumult, clatter, haste, market. All this is for the purpose of depriving the people of these two first basic conditions, and the circumstances in which God could be born. For the same reason its aim is also to stifle in the hearts of people the inherent desire and longing for God.

If a person places a barrier in his own heart to ensure peace, removal and silence, he can live in the world without being harmed by it. Without this barrier he enters into the worldly tumult, and so he is entirely and passionately plunged into it, and this is his ruin. This occurs because there were not the conditions for the birth of the Lord Jesus in his heart. Satan has here a great field for action, and this is his aim.

In giving ourselves to the Mother Most Holy, we give her our souls as a stable, and there she gives birth to the Lord Jesus, and with Saint Joseph and the Angels, watches over His growth.

Everything operates as it was in the actual birth. Precisely for this the soul must have these two conditions of silence and removal. This is the first condition of consecration of self to the Mother of God, and the first effect. If the soul fulfils this first condition, the tumult of the world can be at his side without it causing him any harm, just as it was with the Holy Family in Bethlehem.

`   From such a good undertaking of the act of consecration of self to the Mother of God, and from this message, there must of necessity develop deep true humility. If this is not the result, it means that in the embryo of this consecration of self there is some kind of fundamental want.

The third point of our meditation will be a holy indifference as to what becomes of self. It ensues from this that we give to the Mother Most Holy the power to lead us in the way that she wills. This holy indifference gives the strength of perseverance for every outpost of life, and for every sector of action.

True devotion to the Mother Most Holy is the fulfilment of the command of the Lord Jesus, arising out of the conversation with Mary and Martha, i.e. His reminder: ***"You are troubled about many things, and only one thing is necessary."*** When this condition of consecration of self to the Mother Most Holy is fulfilled, it is all the same whether one is in the part of Mary or Martha. (This means that when we give ourselves to the Mother Most Holy, we no longer need to worry about many things, because the Mother Most Holy will worry about everything for us). From the consecration of self to the Mother Most Holy, there results the perfect giving of self to the Lord Jesus, and unity of self with Him, which is exactly that about which the Lord Jesus spoke when He said that only one thing is necessary. That which determines the goal and the way to Him is the consecration of self to the Mother Most Holy.

32. The Rosary generates saints. It generates saints through those who say it as they ought, and it generates saints through those who say it. For the sake of their prayers, and at my request, God, in omnipotence and mercy, calls saints. Somebody may say: "There were saints before the Rosary came to be." But they had the Rosary mysteries so much in themselves, that is, the mysteries of the Redemption, that they lived with them every moment, and these mysteries led them through death to Heaven. The prayer of their mouths was their constant nourishment, while their countless prayers celebrated on earth are, and endure, in eternity. There is no other way. How few people know this, and it is necessary that everybody should understand that the Rosary through me, is the most direct, the easiest and the most important way to unity with the Lord Jesus, and this is the aim of everything here on earth. It establishes holiness, so that nothing unholy can separate us from the Lord Jesus. The one who loves the Rosary – the Rosary does not disappoint, and the Rosary leads the one who is so faithful to it that he lives with it in every moment of earthly life, to the goal of everlasting happiness.

33. When you take the Rosary in your hands, or when you resolve to say it at an appointed time, be it now or later, simultaneously, there steps forward to counteraction, all the army of evil spirits. Call on my help, clearly realising that that same opportunity to say the Rosary is already a grace. Nobody says "Jesus", only the Holy Spirit, and likewise, nobody says the Rosary, only the Holy Spirit. Therefore, the devils take flight, because there, where the Holy Spirit is, there is no place for them.

Have the mysteries of the Rosary in your hearts, and in your thoughts. Live with them, because it is only by this means, when you will be saying the Rosary with your mouths, that it will be, as it ought to be.

Love people who have a good heart for you; a loving heart, a faithful heart and a simple heart! At the Rosary think often about what kind of Heart mine is. Be clear in every situation and in every matter. Be well decided when you come to consider whether with this or with that my Heart will be gladdened or saddened.

34. What is good is always good, although one would not know from which side to observe it. What is of evil, although perhaps many a time it does not take long to hide itself, but yet for certain, it is also revealed in a sufficient manner. When the attitude of the heart of the people to God is good, everything else will be in its proper place, and nothing will disturb one. On the contrary, if something is disturbed, even though one was to pour on more and more very clear water, it still remains dull. The gauge in this sphere is the Rosary that is well said and lived through. I have spoken once already about how to find a specific place for yourself in each mystery, and how to blend it into your own life. Today is only the confirmation of this, and the assurance that when the Rosary will be said well and lived through then everything will be bright, pure and clear and will be for the greater glory of God. There can never be too much of this meditation in the life of each person, that is, of the Rosary that is said well and lived through.

And now the following request: The most sublime meditations are worth nothing, if from great ascents something does not flow which has a connection with usual, simple, daily life. This is the gauge as to what sort of spirit is directing this contemplation. Without great exposure for some other kind of proof it is possible to show the spirit through its humility, method and action in usual things.

35. If Rosaries are to be what they have to be, they must be different. If they are to be what they ought to be, they must have their own due place. It follows from this that there should be a standard set to the Rosary, which should not become a hindrance to the saying of it. From the one side there is a multitude of facilities, and from the other side there is a multitude of undue scruples. It is possible to say all the decades, not necessarily moving the beads with the fingers, even if one has a Rosary beads with one, but the place which the Rosary has to occupy, among all matters, is most important. The Rosary does not have to be left at the end, because of tiredness or lack of time. It is necessary to respect it for many reasons:

- The Rosary is holy.
- The Rosary is such a very privileged prayer.

- The Rosary comes from the Mother of God, just as the Lord's Prayer comes from the Lord Jesus.
- The Rosary has so many privileges and indulgences from the Church.
- The Rosary is confirmed and commended by the Popes. The Rosary is above all so far-reaching that has been spoken about here, and each of these things suffices more than enough to give to the Rosary a suitable position in each day, and in an entire lifetime.

Neither with the Orders, nor with the clergy, nor with the laity is this as it ought to be. So everybody has to take this into account, and everyone must reform his own life according to the clock of the Rosary. There are, indeed, exceptions everywhere, but as a whole, it has to be otherwise.

36. I am the Queen. The Queen has authority. I have it from The Father, The Son and The Holy Spirit. I have it for the rescue of souls, for the giving of consolation, for the soothing of pains and the healing of wounds, for the imparting of counsel and caution, for the deliverance of souls from the approaching claws of satan, for the raising up from falls, for the suckling of the hungry, for keeping watch, for assisting, for loving, in a word, for that which the loving heart of a mother does, and for this, and in order to get this authority, to possess it and to rule with it, I receive an inconceivable, unspeakable, infinite gift, before which all Heaven bows down in humility and worships the Lord's Name; it is the gift of power over the Heart of the

Son and over the entire Holy Trinity, Who do not refuse me anything for which I ask and entreat.

Rejoice and be glad with me, worshipping and thanking with me and for me.

37. As one plunges the hand into unknown treasure and draws it out full, then in the Divine Light, one considers and knows the worth of what has been drawn out. So what to consider about to day, if not about the Visitation?

The Mother Most Holy kept everything in Her Heart and she did not confide it to anyone. The greeting of St Elizabeth gave the proof that God Himself revealed this mystery to her, and hence this incomparable, inexpressible joy which found an outlet in the Magnificat, which is a hymn of humility and thanksgiving, of adoration and submission, of love and of prophecy. So great is the joy of the Mother Most Holy that the heart of Elizabeth is filled with understanding of Her Immaculate Heart and a perception of the feeling and experience of This Heart. How immensely holy is St. Elizabeth, through the action of the Holy Spirit which made Her a confidant of the Immaculate Heart of the Mother Most Holy.

We ask that St. Elizabeth would pray for us that we might know, love and imitate the Immaculate Heart. Let us ask that she would obtain for us, unceasingly, more and greater perception of the mysteries of God. In conclusion, let us thank the Lord God for the Graces bestowed on the Immaculate Heart of the Mother of God, and for the graces bestowed on St. Elizabeth through the Nativity.

38. The Assumption is the coronation of "Full of Grace", the announcement of which the Mother Most Holy received at the Annunciation. The Assumption is a stone of offense for unbelievers and dissenters. Therefore this truth of faith was proclaimed as a dogma, and so you should meditate on it in every Rosary in order to convince yourself, because the memory of this dogma and loving it with all your heart is necessary for you, and also it will, before long, become a necessity, because it gives the graces for survival. The thought of Heaven – holy hope, and the example of how, after such suffering and sacrifice, Mary received there Her own place and authority – this will soon be the indispensable line of rescue over the precipice of despair, which will swallow those who do not have it, because they do not wish to have it.

All of the third part of the Holy Rosary, the glorious mysteries, permits all who are saying the Rosary in the Holy Spirit, to comprehend the Will of God, to surrender themselves to it, and to survive and save themselves in it.

Satan knows what the Rosary is, and what it has to be, for the people, and therefore, he orders those who are united with him to throw it away.

39. Advent, Advent, Advent. Great concentration, earnest desire, and deep longing, all enfolded in the most ardent love: all this must be reflected in the quantity and kind of your Rosaries. The Word lived for nine months in the Womb of Mary, and from the first moment everything was accomplished. In the Rosary you have to apply each mystery to the first, or to carry across the first mystery to each of the mysteries – it amounts to the same. Through contemplation of The Word Incarnate in the Womb of Mary, and from living through all of the mysteries of the Redemption in closest union with the first mystery, it will be very easy for you to know and to fathom the humility of the Mother and Son – the humility of the King and Queen – and it will be also easy for you to know in truth the value of the secret of obscurity in the God of Life. The world does not know this and it does not wish that souls would know it, because this would be its defeat. Victory is yours in the Rosary – through living it and saying it.

40.   You are all oppressed because of your admission of God. The weapon and the power, the salvation, the protection and the hope has to be always, and in everything, The Immaculate Heart of Mary, and the key to opening it for the outflow of Graces is the Rosary. It is necessary then to say it perseveringly in faith and hope, and with understanding and will. Maybe there will follow an attack on the consolation and sweetness in prayer, which people so desire. He who is not armed with the Rosary, girdled with the Rosary, supported by the Rosary, and purified by the Rosary must not think that it is possible for him to come forward and do battle with satan, but from the one who is armed, girdled, supported and purified by the Rosary there goes out such brilliance that it hits at the evil spirits. To know about this suffices to have always, and in everything, peace. Then it becomes: *"My peace I give you, My peace I leave with you, not as the world gives do I give to you."*

Let not your hearts be troubled. Do not fear. Believe in Me, and believe in My Mother.

41.   The Holy Spirit looks for the one in whom He may repose. The Holy Spirit acts with sudden force, and the first dwelling place of the Holy Spirit is in the simple and humble souls, who are obedient, who long for Him and who are united with Mary. These are the conditions, which enable Him to act. The Holy Spirit is not adored and worshipped properly, but the more there is of good and praiseworthy Rosaries the greater will be the devotion to the Holy Spirit, Who is there present in the thirteenth mystery. It is necessary to find a place for the Holy Spirit in each mystery of the Holy Rosary: in the Annunciation, the Magnificat of the Visitation and so on in all the fifteen mysteries.

    You know a lot about the Holy Rosary, but now you have to find out other things about it, but blessed are those who have not discovered and do not know everything about it, but believe. If knowledge and exposure of the secretiveness of the mysteries of the Rosary disposes many to this devotion and corrects many, then my desires, if only in part, will be satisfied, and my Heart consoled.

42.   The Rosary is still not always what it has to be, what it ought to be, in our life. It is necessary to pray about saying the Rosary well, because this is a grace. The Rosary is so important – the importance of which we do not know – that even if in a small way people guessed at it, **they**

The SECRET POWER of the ROSARY

would be praying that life would be about the saying of the Rosary. We would be praying earnestly about this.

The Rosary has to regenerate the world. The Rosary has to unite the open earth with Heaven, and the inhabitants of the earth with each other, as with a great fire. The Rosary makes the greatest recompense in Heaven and it effects the greatest appreciation of, and gratitude to, those who say it on earth. Wherever the Rosary is said there is drawn the special protection and speedy help of those who are in Heaven. With the **greatest** joy in union with that which the first Ave brought to Mary, they are repeating: "Ave! Ave! Ave Maria!"

It is necessary to remember that moments on earth are precious, and should not be given into the sack of the thief. It is also necessary to be sensitive in prayer, because then it will be easy to differentiate – and it is necessary to wish to differentiate in each moment – and the reason it will be easy is because the one is a grace and the other is a temptation; one is from God and the other is from satan. All of this is a fight, and the Rosary assures the victory. If people would say the Rosary as they should, they would not commit so many errors. All evil is the error flowing out from fraud.

Everyone must offer sacrifices – not only the children of Fatima. There are souls who agonise about what to give as a sacrifice for the Lord Jesus and His Mother, and there is nothing that would be more pleasing and easy for an offering than a particular decade of the Rosary. Already you know much about the Rosary. Behold how the Mother of God accepted the greeting from Her Own little daughter, Bernadette, and how She said with her: "Glory be to the

Father." May you know the Rosary, pray it, encourage others to do so, and gain the victory through the saying of the Rosary.

May She be greeted: Full of Grace, Queen of the Universe, Lady and Mother of each and everyone, Mother of Mercy weeping over the world, over that which threatens it, over lost souls, over the insult of the Majesty of God, over the waste of the Passion of Her Son and of the Redemption, over the waste of time and Grace, over the mysterious passing on of so many souls in every moment, not to a blessed, but to a terrible eternity.

Look intently at Her. Have Her feelings, Her thoughts, and Her desires in mind and in memory, in feeling, in heart and in will, and say the Rosary. Amen.

43. I ask that the Mother of God, in this meditation, would give us an indication as to what to do in order make a reality the wish expressed by Jesus: *"I came to start a fire on earth, and how I wish that that it was blazing."*

In every mystery of the Rosary this desire to enkindle the fire is present. Behold the first mystery, the Annunciation, when this mysterious fire inflamed the Immaculate Heart, and the Archangel Gabriel and Heaven saw it, and wondered. In the second mystery inflamed with this fire, is the heart of St. Elizabeth who proclaimed the words which still endure and will endure forever: *"Blessed art Thou among women!"* And inflamed with this fire, the heart of the father Zechariah sings the Canticle – the hymn which endures in the Church in the mouths and the hearts of Priests and Monks and many others, because it is still in the breviary. This fire purified the heart of St. John, and this fire touched those who pensively said: "What then will this child be?" For the Hand of the Lord was with him. And so on in each mystery: *"I came to start a fire on earth, and how I wish that it was blazing."* Therefore, He became a Child, which the Love of God gave to the shepherds, and to the Three Kings. In many hearts the fire was inflamed and in many – it was not.

The Divine Child lit the fire of His Own Divine Love in the hearts of two prophets, Simeon and Anna, but in many others it was not enkindled. The Divine Child desired to inflame the hearts of the princes of the Church. This was why He was in the temple among them, but they were not inflamed.

May this desire of the Heart of the Lord Jesus: *"I came to start a fire on earth, and how I wish that it was blazing"*, become the most fervent of our hearts' desires, which will regulate every vital matter. Then later, in the examination of conscience, it is necessary to consider what one has done during the day just ending towards this purpose, that this fire would be inflamed, and whether the intention was in work as well as in suffering.

44. God gave Mary to us, and Mary gave the Rosary to us. This is our way to God. Today let us consider that we give particular joy to the Lord God in the One Holy Trinity, when we express our devotion and praise of Mary with, precisely, the Rosary.

The rhythm of the Rosary, when said in common, is not an indifferent thing. Just as rhythm acts with great strength on the material, even to the bursting of a strong construction, likewise in the sphere of the spiritual, the saying of the Rosary in common has an equivalent action to this.

45. In the Rosary the pronunciation of the name of Mary and the name of Jesus must be done differently from what is now being done by many people. It must be in conscious knowledge – even though this would be limited – of who Mary is and who Jesus is. It is necessary to stand in the presence of God, and, in the same way as the usual rules, lovingly and with deepest reverence to keep one's thoughts on the mystery and to pronounce, particularly piously, the most holy name of Jesus and the holy name of Mary.

Very often it is necessary to become aware of one's own life, and to compare it with the life of the Divine Child and of His Mother, and then to offer it to the Immaculate Heart of Mary, and through Her to the Most Holy Trinity.

Oh that people would know what the saying of the fifteen decades of the Rosary means! They would not start anything before saying them. But the understanding and acceptance of this requires an act of faith, that it is so, because the Mother Most Holy says that it is so.

The triumph of the Immaculate is so near … it is necessary to reflect on it in the two last mysteries.

It may happen that there is absolutely no time to say all the fifteen mysteries. It is good then, in turn, to say a given mystery, to dwell on it for a moment in thought and in heart, and in this way to go through all the fifteen, and the love, which will be in this, brings about further graces for the good saying of the Rosary. For example, when I am hurrying to work in the morning, I try in thought to go over all the fifteen mysteries, and already in a certain way they are penetrating into me, and later on, at a convenient time I say the Rosary, either all at once or in parts, or even in decades.

Mother Most Holy, I am pleased with your triumph, your glory; that you are Queen of the universe, and Queen over everything that came from the Hand of the Eternal Father.

A way of interior life: one takes one mystery for one day, (for example the first) and lives with it, and then gives everything, all prayers, matters, and sacrifices to the Mother of God in the mystery of the Annunciation – to this most pure, humble, silent and Most Prayerful Virgin, Whose Immaculate Heart completes love and longing for God.

Then on the second day one should offer everything to the Mother Most Holy who in the second mystery performs acts of self-sacrifice, labour, silence and humility to the highest degree; who is full of obscurity in this mystery, but also full of the highest happiness, pouring out Her Soul in the hymn of thanksgiving, mentioning consciously the greatness of the gifts of God, in the Magnificat.

The third day should to be lived through in the same way, uniting with the third mystery, and so on. By this means we unite with the call of the Mother Most Holy: "I am all in the Rosary; there you will find me".

Now we already know how it goes, and how to draw with joy from the mysteries of the Rosary, which are the greatest gift. You will be drawing with joy from the source of the Saviour. This source is the ever-pure water, ever fresh, and always gushing, *to form the new person in Mary.*

As with matter, which can be condensed drop by drop until all is soaking with water, so the Rosary has to penetrate us and completely pervade us. Of what is the life of people, always and everywhere composed? It is family, work, and one's attitude to God, to people and to one's own soul. Would then that it might be so: *live now, not I – there lives in me the mysteries of the Rosary of Jesus and Mary.*

46. Meditation comes from:
- the intention,
- the setting aside of time for it,
- the coming, in much humility, to stand at the foot of the throne of the Mother Most Holy, the moment, when in concentration, we wait in expectation of understanding of the kind that is awakened in mind and heart (and this is so with every mystery on which we meditate) and then acceptance without hesitation or grimace of what was suggested by the Holy Guardian Angel.

I am taking the first and last mystery. Servant and Queen: What is this saying to us? The Mother of God is the same in the first mystery as in the fifteenth, only that in the first we have Her will, Her action, and in the fifteenth Her acceptance of reward.

The Annunciation and Coronation are like two clasps which close everything. Placing oneself at the feet of the Mother of God, and having named the mystery, remaining thus and giving time to this *is the beginning.* But for the end of the meditation let us do this: if we have received some light or resolution let us give thanks, but if they are not present let us also give thanks, and let us not compare this with other ways and means of meditation.

The Mother of God has a great simplicity of faith. She is, as it were, penetrated with this faith, and has a feeling of awe in the presence of the Archangel Gabriel. With contemplation of the penetration of the Mother of God with this virtue, with this faith and desire for the Salvation, we become completely acquainted with Her, and this is the starting point of the Rosary. The Mother of God had only one momentary fear. When She got confirmation from the Angel Her faith became still greater and fuller. And still, though She had full faith, in some most wonderful, but for us, a not understood way, it increased. When She questioned, made sure and knew that there was nothing unworthy in the Virginal Wedding, then She accepted the Will of God. Here is inherent all the mystery of the action of the Mother of God through Her revelation: a person can have doubts, but these doubts must be from fear of God; from fear of rejecting what comes from God, and at the same time from fear of succumbing to illusion, to error or to evil. This establishes precisely one thing: fear of God and fear of evil, but they are, as it were, separated. Fear of God is in the foreground. The doubt has to endure for a certain, definite short time, varying for different people, but enduring until there is knowledge of the truth. From the moment when one knows that this is from God, it must be absolutely accepted. "Behold the handmaid of the Lord." Other attitudes there dare not be! In Her revelations the Mother of

God brings the Will of God. In other words, God makes known His Will through the Mother of God, or through the Angels.

And here is the turning point: – the outpouring of these graces upon us depends upon our reception of such revelations – *"He who is from God hears the words of God"*. Those who are accepting the desires of the Mother of God are changing life. Therefore, how terrible is this testing of the desires of the Mother of God (La Salette, Lourdes, Fatima and others), because here is the Will of God given to the world through the Mother of God, and confirmed by the Popes, which establishes great facilitation.

This is a primary attitude for those who wish to be the servants, children and slaves of the Mother Most Holy. Otherwise they can become neither slaves or children, or even servants.

Blessed are you who believed – this is the theme of the second mystery and has to link with the fifteenth in which we see the reward of the Mother Most Holy for this, Her faith, because with God not one word is impossible. We have, therefore, to expect the results of this blessing that we have believed. This is particularly important and because it points at what St. Louis Marie Grignon de Montfort proposes: *"with Mary, in Mary, through Mary and for Mary."* In other words our behaviour cannot differ from Mary's behaviour.

In the Gospel the Lord Jesus gave us a test – the one who is from God hears the Words of God. This test can be applied to knowledge of the Gospel, the teaching of the

The SECRET POWER of the ROSARY

Catholic faith, the revelations of the Mother of God, or a command from the Pope, and therefore, all these are means that the Lord God gives us to hear His Own Voice and His Own Will.

The fifteenth mystery

This call, endures as it were, forever: *"Come My Bride! My Beautiful! My Beloved! You will be crowned". "They bring to the King virgins for Her, they bring them with merriment..."* 'Virgins', this means chaste souls, chastened by means of love.

47. The kingdom of Mary is within you.

It is necessary, by means of the Rosary, to widen, deepen, prioritize, and purify the kingdom of Mary. There is still time. It is important that, most of all, prayer and desire would unite as many souls as possible in this kingdom of Mary. To remember continually, that one belongs to this kingdom, that one widens and deepens it, that in it and with it, one acts with Jesus, Who wishes to honour His Own Mother, establishes the spring of unspeakable happiness, which we ought to feel. The feeling of happiness from belonging to the kingdom of Mary grows, already, here on earth. One ought to exact from this feeling that one is already united, here and now, with those who are establishing the kingdom of Mary in Heaven. The Mother Most Holy, as Queen, has already carried the victory, because this was given to her in the promise, when she was in the Mind of the Father: victory by the Power of God accomplished through Mary.

Here I wish to speak about something very important, but it is very difficult. I do not know if I will succeed. It is necessary to differentiate the Kingdom of Mary from the Kingdom of Jesus, which is the only one, and yet it is not the only one. The Kingdom of Mary is something that forms, comes into existence, and which is the action, the gaining and, as it were, the conquest of new territories and new attainments with the minimum of energies and measures. There were, and there are, such victories in your kingdom, granted through Her after entreating Her for them, when many a time a handful of valiant ones conquered, with great might, the enemy of the Cross and your enemies. They had full consciousness of this, both they who experienced this victory, and also those who recognised it, and gratitude for this is expressed forever in the Mass of thanksgiving for the chocimskie victory. It contains in itself, as it were, thanksgiving for bygone, as well as later, miracles of Mary, which were achieved in chivalry in the nation, and later in Vienna. This spirit we should take to heart.

Here it is about our own consciousness, and that of all people, of the importance of everything done in the service of the Queen. The meaning of this is that for every word of prayer, little mortification, and sacrificial intention the Mother of God, in response and through the power of Christ carries great conquests; snatching back souls who have come close to the precipice. There is still a lack of this with us, and it is necessary also to give this to another in such a way that pride would not arise: *this is what I can,* but only, these are great matters.

Christ's Kingdom is apparently the same, and yet, with it, there is still a certain difference: - there is the flood of the power and the mercy of the merits of the Redemption on those whom Mary has gathered, and places before her Son, certain that He will not refuse her. So this is, as it were, the next stage. Both kingdoms are still completely united with each other, which establishes the mystery which – whether through humility or through the deepest silence, or through the outpouring of the Magnificat – has to glorify God in union with the Angels who, together with the Saints do, only, this for all eternity. This gives the beginning of the faint taste of eternal happiness.

48. I am the Most Holy Virgin of The Rosary: *I came to remind humanity to change their lives and not to make God sad with the weight of sins. People are to say the Rosary and do penance for sins.* All this was told by the Mother of God in Fatima. The Most Holy Virgin wishes that people would say the Rosary. She has a right to all their Rosaries, and she has the right to do with them what she wishes.

The Annunciation: This is the preparation for each way that God wishes to lead us.

The Visitation: All housework is sanctified though the fulfilment of it through The Mother Most Holy, either at one's one place or at a relative's place.

The Birth of God: This is association in solitude with Jesus.

The Presentation: This is, as it were, the second stage of the first mystery.

The Finding in the Temple: This is the life of The Holy Family.

And now it is necessary to realise that in the present life we have a denial of all of these mysteries. The world with full consciousness fights against these mysteries. By diverting people it succeeds in tearing them away in immense measure. The first mystery is fought against through the personal I; that is personal plans such as "How I can effect the world my own way". The second mystery also is fought against through the great development of this 'me', so that I do not see others. They do not interest me. The third mystery is fought against through the fact that my great important 'me' must overflow itself outside in association with the world. The combating of the fourth mystery occurs when that my 'me' is so great that it does not wish to drop even the least thing in sacrifice but only to seize everything for self. The Finding and the plan of life of the Holy Family is combated through the assertion that this important 'me' neither seeks God – because everywhere and in everything it seeks only self – nor will it wear any shackles, even family life.

This complete meditation and drawing of comparisons can be entitled: THE ROSARY AND THE WORLD.

In the Rosary it is possible to find power and victory over all these temptations.

In the sorrowful part of the Rosary there is the battle with that with which the world draws and ruins us. That is, about sensuality – it's use and its misuse. From the attitude of the world there flows out disgust for penance, and fear of suffering. It is necessary, therefore, to enlighten people about that to which the world is reduced though lack of the Rosary.

The SECRET POWER of the ROSARY

The Rosary has to soak into us from childhood, acting invisibly, and drawing down graces. It does not suffice to say the Rosary; it is necessary to be brought up according to the Rosary, and to create a completely new ideal, because the Rosary educates by forming entirely different ideals.

Behold we are seeing what the world has come to through neglect of the Rosary, and though the substitution of it with stopgaps.

It would never have been like this if the Rosary had been said, as the Mother Most Holy desired, and as the Popes commanded, exhorted, and warned.

49.   The Rosary is the treasure of Heaven and earth.

The Rosary contains in itself everything that is necessary; when the Mother Most Holy calls us to do penance, the Rosary fulfils this. It is with no other prayer, only with the Rosary, that the Mother Most Holy bids us to pray.

The Rosary is distinctly, and without any doubt, the will of the Mother Most Holy. It is her request, her recommendation and her command, under threat.

The Rosary teaches us to live as is necessary.

The Rosary gives the strength and grace in order to live as is necessary.

The Rosary makes the crooked path straight.

The Rosary assures that death is as a passage to Heaven.

May is mine. Yes, the Mother Most Holy got it from her Son. Would that you would accept the excess of its consequential graces.

BARBARA KLOSS

The Rosary – is the unending instruction about the perfections of the Most Holy Trinity, and about its action. Just as one ought not to go to work without a meal – the want of it would reveal itself in physical weakness – so it is not possible without the saying of the Rosary to think about any sort of action with success. Through the Rosary one enters into unity with the Holy Trinity.

They say that there is never enough of Mary. You have to know that Mary never has enough of the Rosary from you.

There is no need to guess what the Rosary does and where it reaches. Every child, when he says it piously, is a representative of all of us. This is because there exists a great solidarity of sinners. One does not say: "pray for me a sinner", but "for us sinners", and then this is poured out on everyone. If it were, that the Rosary was woven from a great many prayers, then it would not be so attainable for everybody.

As one selects something (for example, from the earth) it is possible to choose from a wide area, and it will be shallow, and it is also possible to narrow down this area and then to reach deeply. The prayers, Our Father and Hail Mary, are like a handrail. Thought, heart, and words have to keep the details of the mysteries. If somebody keeps the thought on the mysteries, and most piously says the prayers – such a one will be astonished with his own knowledge. He will be able to tell himself: "I know, and I have certainty."

The Annunciation contains in itself the fullness of all the virtues of the Mother Most Holy, which are revealed outwardly in the other mysteries. So in the fourteen mysteries that follow nothing surprises one any longer, as there is only in the heart, with Divine clarity, the radiated truth of the first mystery.

Let the Most Holy Child Jesus, Himself, teach you of the love in the pronunciation of this word "Mother" and how the word "Mother" was bestowed. This word is continually repeated: Holy Mary, Mother of God, pray for us sinners now and at the hour of our death.

These are short thoughts which help to realise that which the Lord Jesus wished, i.e. that His Mother would be better known and loved. (Told in Fatima).

When will people return to paying attention to these simple things? They are satisfied to look at the Rosary as something which is perhaps for other people, but not for themselves, because a multitude of people, in their own blindness maintain that "the Rosary is good for these or those people, but not for me."

The Rosary is the measure of the standard of orthodoxy. Every heresy, from the very beginning recoils from it.

The Rosary produces interior discipline, develops, forms and strengthens character.

The Rosary is a bundle of the love of all Christians in the world, and the sign by which they discern the true children of God and Mary from one end of the earth to the other.

The Rosary is the sweetest keepsake, which, with the blessing of Father and Mother, each one takes for life, even to the coffin.

The Rosary is the great gift, the great coin, although it is changed for small pennies. Like a little child, who comes to buy a kilo of sweets for two pennies, and even though he has no more money, someone pays for it, saying: "Let him have these sweets." The Mother of God intercedes for the one who brings his own little Rosary. This is a special economy.

The Rosary must be vocal and is not to be said only in thought. This would not be the Rosary. Whether in silent whisper, or, said aloud, or sung, it goes into Heaven and endures there forever, and becomes joined to the songs of the Angels.

The Rosary is this long-lasting, suffering and persevering knock, which has the certainty of opening the door.

The Rosary is the powerful acknowledgement of faith, which pronounces that Mary is the Mother of God, full of grace, united with God, and is our Mediatrix, whose prayer and mediation is necessary for us for every moment of life and death.

The Rosary is the Most Holy Mother's continuous constrictive action that obliterates the head of the serpent, which lies in wait for her children, and it is the unceasing link between the Old Testament and the New.

The Rosary is the slogan with which to combat, and which has the certainty of victory. Amen. As the Creed is, this is.

50. The Annunciation was at night time. The prayers of the Mother Most Holy were extended. Night prayers – this is penance.

In the second mystery we have the penance of the Mother Most Holy during her difficult journey in the heat on the mountain, as well as in the work she did at St. Elizabeth's. Then there is the great penance of the Mother Most Holy in homelessness at the Birth, in great weariness, in annoyances from the people in Bethlehem. These tribulations and all kinds of suffering from people, accompanied the Mother Most Holy from childhood until her greatest shame as Mother of the Condemned. The penance of the Mother Most Holy existed, therefore, in the Joyful Mysteries. The greatest happiness of the night of Bethlehem, still was penance. Then followed the penance of the Mother Most Holy in the pilgrimage to the temple for purification. Although there was joy in the pilgrimage to the temple of Jerusalem, this was later followed by the pain of losing the Lord Jesus – penance.

The complete life spent in Nazareth flows in great simplicity, in the greatest happiness from unity with God; but there is also penance there, because the Mother Most Holy had in herself the most perfect spirit of penance, and this was to God, extraordinarily pleasing.

In the second part of the Rosary (the sorrowful mysteries) it is necessary to enter into this great penance of the Mother Most Holy, which she united with the penance of her Son.

Everything, which people have to bear and suffer, they have to call penance, and to accept such penance. The Mother Most Holy said this in Fatima, but already before this, she demonstrated it with all of her own life, but people do not know how to read this book. Therefore, everything, which is connected with our life, and the inevitable, should be called penance, and it should be accepted as such. When one has the understanding that this is penance, all these troubles of the present time change into joy, inasmuch as it becomes evident that the penance is not worthy of the future glory.

For this, however, it is necessary to have in one's own heart the totality of the Rosary strongly engraved, and particularly the tenth, eleventh and twelfth mysteries, as these give an understanding of the sense of everything. Because people do not have this understanding, people do not offer life as penance. Everything is in the Rosary, but it is necessary to know the Mother of God more and more. This is very simple and easy to relate to children and to grown-ups alike, but it is necessary to repeat it over and over, because this is really necessary for people, and by this means they will easily take it in.

51. I wish to sow the Rosary in the whole world, but about this – my sowing – as in the Gospels, there is carried on the unceasing struggle. In this sowing of mine a multitude of people can take a share, and each one can co-operate as far as he can manage, and with as much as he can afford.

The measure of service is:
- as in everything – love,
- as in everything – purity of intention,
- as in everything – the degree of self-giving,

only in this matter the measure is faith in the truth of my words, and in the importance and efficacy of the Rosary. In this is humility and obedience.

It is necessary to say the Rosary, to have the Rosary about oneself, to revere the Rosary, and to live it in such a way that people would see this, because there are some people who are ashamed, in the face of the world, to even carry the beads on themselves.

The first part of the Joyful Mysteries is the introduction to the mystery of the life of the Mother Most Holy with God, from the union in the mystery of the Incarnation – from which flows and in which dwells all the fifteen mysteries – up to her reign over all the universe. The beginning of all this is the Fiat of the first mystery, and this has to determine today's meditation:

What sort of place has it in our life?

What is this Fiat?

To what does it lead?

Mother Most Holy, we beseech thee, give us, through the Rosary, a share in your magnificent Fiat.

52.   The Lord Jesus said about Himself:
   " I am the way, the truth and the life."
One goes the way, one proceeds with the truth, and one attains the life; but how to live, how to go the way through life from the temporal to the eternal, how to absorb the truth – to nourish oneself with it, to suffer for it, to fight for it and to die for it – how to enter Heaven, how to adore God's glory, and how to live truly in Mary, with Mary, through Mary and for Mary forever – this, the Rosary shows us.

This means that one would flow into the harbour of salvation quickly and without any deviation. This is possible to achieve only through well-said Rosaries, well lived-through Rosaries, and the acceptance of the Rosary with all of one's heart.

53.   The Mother Most Holy, flowing over with immense graces, sings her hymn of adoration and love, and she sings for a long time before her own way of the Cross. Although we do not hear it, this hymn endures through all the mysteries, in the same way as the Fiat. The Mother Most Holy sings the hymn Magnificat, which is the most beautiful hymn – with the most beautiful voice – of adoration of God that was ever heard on earth. We have to do the same. We have to unite with it. This is easy, only one should arrange it in love, so that with this Magnificat in every moment of life and death there would be no difficulty or constraint, but rather that it should flow from the abundance of a loving heart. If, in suffering, we sing the Magnificat, together with the Fiat, it has a most wonderful sound, in which God Himself in the Most Holy Trinity is pleased. Through uniting the voice of our hearts with the voice of the Immaculate Heart of Mary, it takes on the values of horrifying hell and of enrapturing Heaven.

54.   **"A***nd they saw no one, only Jesus Himself***"** – this is from the transfiguration of the Lord on the mountain. This was not imagined by each of the apostles; they really saw this, and later they no longer saw it. It was only for this moment that Moses and Elijah became visible to them.

It is the same with the Grace of God. It draws near. It is real, and after this it becomes the footprint of this grace that was, but at the same time, it leaves a great strengthening of hope. This means, that we who experience so much evidence of the action of grace – so extraordinary – should remember that when this grace is withdrawn and darkness comes, the memory of it strengthens our faith and confirms in us, peace. One should remember all of this.

The Mother Most Holy in all of the mysteries of the Rosary gives us the former and the latter. She gives us a tangible experience of grace, and at the same time she strengthens us in the darkness of the time when we do not feel this grace. This grace is contained in the mysteries, but many do not feel it, and then there is the appearance of ineffectiveness, but in every mystery, when one does not see the same grace, one should see the Mother of God. *Lifting up their eyes they saw no one, only the same Jesus.*

After great graces it may seem as if there were a deprivation of them, but we must believe that the Mother of God is present.

55.   In order to love me, it is necessary to know me. In order to know me it is necessary to say the Rosary. In order to be pleasing to me it is necessary to live through the mysteries of the Rosary with me. In order to have this grace it is necessary to say the Rosary. This closes the circle, and then all my promises for the saying of the Rosary are fulfilled.

It is necessary to say the Rosary with love – this means to say it the best way; and with humility – this means with a feeling of unworthiness and shame, so that it is a call to unite one's own poor Rosaries with the most beautiful crowns of Roses which, for generations, have been offered to me by my faithful slaves, by my children, by my servants and by my courtiers.

In each mystery there is compassionate love and mercy upon you, and for you, and through reflecting on this in the fifteen mysteries the true devotion to the Divine Mercy is celebrated, and thus let it be.

56.   I am with you. Often I am looking, and looking with sorrow. The struggles not supported by the Rosary are without fruit. (They can be fruitful for those who have good will, even though they know nothing about the Rosary).

I am the Mother Most Holy of the Rosary, and of the victory. One is followed by the other; the title only is twofold. My victory is the power of the merits of my Son. It was promised and accomplished, and fulfils itself in time. Let you gather my words and instructions, and pass them on to others, so that not even a basketful of fragments remains. This is my command.

Whoever hopes in me will not be confused. Believe in the Divine Power; believe in me, because on It, in It, for It and through It I wield everything.

Let every Hail Mary from now on become laden with a declaration of love. In the meditations, link often the first mystery with the fifteenth, and the fifteenth with the first. There is no other way. I have told you this, and once more I repeat it: There is no other way like the way, which my Son, Himself, has walked. To me He extended the greatest grace through leading me this same way, and I am inviting you on it.

The SECRET POWER of the ROSARY

Waking in the morning let you be pleased that you have still another possibility of saying the Rosary well, and let you strive towards this. In me and through me all matters, even little things, witness to the service of God. Otherwise, even the most toilsome day is a nonsensical effort.

57. The Holy Spirit is the Spirit of Love, Peace and Merriment. The Mother Most Holy possesses it to the most perfect degree, and it is precisely through the Rosary that the Mother Most Holy desires to pass on these graces of the Holy Spirit to us. Here, the statement that he who asks receives, is realised. The request in each Hail Mary is pleasing to Almighty God, because it is conveyed – if it is well-conveyed, i.e. in the complete giving of self to Mary and through Mary, and if it is conveyed with faith, and based on the acknowledgement of one's own infirmity. On the one hand there should be acknowledgement of one's own infirmity, and on the other hand there should be trust. O that you would know what happens, when, at your request here, the Mother Most Holy intercedes for you. After naming the mystery, and after saying the decade with the intention of beseeching, nothing else remains, only to adore the Holy Trinity, which is in the words of the "Glory be to the Father".

Behold how the saying of the Rosary appears. This "Glory be to the Father" applies also to a better understanding of the Mother of God. When we say "Glory be to the Father" we are considering how perfectly the Mother Most Holy gives glory to the Holy Trinity, and we understand the Mother of God better.

58. The Mother of God would be very pleased if, when saying the Rosary and reflecting on it, that there would be a continual return to these words: "Look My daughter, at this Heart surrounded with thorns, with which ungrateful people wound me every moment, through blasphemies and ingratitude. You, at least, try to console me, and announce in my name that I will come at the hour of death, with the necessary graces for salvation for all those, who on the first Saturday of five consecutive months go to confession, receive Holy Communion, say the Rosary, and keep me company while meditating on the mysteries of the Rosary with the intention of making reparation". (On the 10.12.1925 the Mother Most Holy revealing herself to Sister Lucy showed her, her own Heart surrounded with thorns and said that which is above. From the book *"Our regeneration in the Heart of Mary"* Karmel. Poznan 1947).

This sorrowful complaint from the revelation of Fatima is to be taken as a meditation with all of the mysteries. Even though one would not have any other meditation on the individual mysteries, and only kept a thought on this, which the Lord Jesus wishes, i.e. that this Heart would be loved more, this would suffice.

This Heart, which through its own love and longing brought down the Saviour to the world is this same Heart, which with such great deep and hidden joy hurries to St. Elizabeth, and there finds knowledge and understanding of His mystery, and also immense joy through discovering that there is on earth a second heart who recognised this Immaculate Heart, who understood and loved it, and who, in praise of God and His Laws, united with it. This St. Elizabeth is a great saint. This is a very great saint, and it is possible to take her to oneself as a patron, who will obtain graces for us, by her entreaty, and will lead us on to have greater and greater knowledge of the Immaculate Heart of Mary, which is what the Lord Jesus desires. It is necessary to unite this desire of the Lord Jesus with the individual mysteries of the Rosary, and when we are doing this what happens is that our hearts are astonished and extended ....

The heart of St. Elizabeth, through the Holy Spirit, had its own particular understanding and knowledge of the Immaculate Heart of Mary, which is the abyss, which is filled up to the brim with God.

The desire which we ought to have, and which ought to completely absorb us, is the desire for knowledge of this Heart, and it is necessary to show this desire to others, to encourage them to have it, and also to make it easier for them to fill up other hearts through guiding them in this direction. Then, even if everything was demolished and even if all the evil spirits were unchained, as we are seeing happening, we will have this peace, which the world cannot give.

I am now only just beginning to comprehend how great is the power of this Heart and the kind of control it has, through inexpressible humility, over the Divine Heart and over human hearts. Through the incorporation of one or the other of the sayings of Fatima (e.g. "Look, my daughter .... Jesus desires ...."") in each particular mystery, is to extend, exceedingly, the outflow of graces.

Not to look around, but only to that one desire, and through this to give homage to the Lord Jesus through obedience to His Will.

59. It is not possible to disregard the Rosary. A waste of Rosary graces is a waste of great graces. Direction of thought to one of the mysteries of the Rosary is the shortest and the strongest connection line with the Heavenly harbour. I have thrown out this line many times to you people. How very many are thankful that through this they can have my help. What great graces I confer on those who trust in me. It is necessary to acknowledge the Rosary. It is necessary to deepen humility in the mysteries and to draw nourishment and strength from them. It is necessary to love the Rosary in order to live with it, because from all of my promises there issues one: that living with the Rosary one experiences life well, and living well with the Rosary – one will be saved.

O the Rosary wages a struggle. Does it surprise anybody that when all the mysteries are taken together, and each one individually, it shows the struggle against satan and against all hell, as well as a means of conquering him? Few realise – even those who say the Rosary well and piously – that in the first mystery is contained that which is necessary to know about the means of my struggle and my victory over satan and hell. Through the most humble humiliation and supplication of the Divine Majesty for the Saviour of the world, through the FIAT, through the mystery of the Incarnation, through the loving adoration of the Will of God, through silence and a hidden life of prayer and work – is to become acquainted with that with which one conquers the world.

So it is possible for many to uncover the truth and the law, because such are the laws of this struggle, and it is necessary to adore God in the victory given to me. God desired it thus, and not otherwise – to defeat him through me; his greatest ruination in such a victory. So it is necessary to speak, to know, and to pray about this in the Rosary, because each mystery is the knowledge of the truth, and of the law of the struggle against satan, and of the victory over him. To join in this, to glorify God in this and to ask for imitation, for the acquirement of virtues – that is, of a constant disposition, because the struggle is constant, not ceasing for even a moment, until death.

In such a way to go over the particular mysteries, e.g. the sixth: With what does the Lord Jesus conquer satan? It is not by leading down hosts of Angels for His Own defense, but through the torture of the Agony in the Garden, and later through the bloody sacrifice for sinners, and through the adoration of the Father with the most splendid, most painful, most victorious prayer, in the greatest humility and obedience: ***"Father if You wish, take this chalice from Me; nevertheless, not My will, but Thy will be done."*** (Luke. 22, 42).

People are saying the Rosary in the hope that they will obtain, through constant entreaties, e.g. health or something else, and they do not understand that this is a struggle. There is not an understanding in the Church that this is a struggle, that it is necessary for people to prepare for the struggle, that it is necessary for them to arm, that it is necessary to instruct them about this fight, and that it is necessary to draw out the graces of victory for the struggle, through uniting and imitating that which is contained in each mystery.

60.   I am completely in the Rosary. Seek me there; find me there, and there also find my Heart.

The Heart of the Mother of God is easy to find, to know and to imitate. Only in the heart, and nowhere else, is located the entire attitude to God and to all creatures. As a human heart is, so it is. One does not say that since a human being has reason and education – that it is the same in the moral sense, because this is not true, since these are inessential things.

The Heart of the Mother of God is so immense, because such an overflowing of immense graces dwell in It. In every mystery one sees it, only it is from a different angle, and in the complete Rosary one can look back at It.

If one says to somebody, that he has a lack of heart, people do not desire him. They move away from such a person, even though he would have, I do not know how many, diplomas. On the miraculous medal there are two Hearts – the Heart of the Mother of God nearby the Heart of the Lord Jesus – and this is a symbol of the most splendid love of the Heart of the most perfect creature to the Creator.

It is necessary thus to understand It, thus to venerate It, and thus to love It, so that there would not be present the underlying greatest danger – and I repeat the greatest danger – which is that of a heart turned towards itself, but rather that it would effect the greatest joy to the Divine Heart of the Lord Jesus, which is what He desires.

The world regenerates itself through the Rosary. The Rosary changes the hearts of the people. The Rosary protects thought and action from the approach of satan. The Rosary purifies. The Rosary conquers. In it is the Heart of the Mother of God. Mary has given the Rosary many times as a gift from her Immaculate Heart.

61.   October is the month of Mary.

October is the month of the Rosary.

October is the month of the assembling and the storing of graces, which will act later. To those children who are near to the Heart of the Mother, October gives a sense of joy and the power of this effect.

October has to be utilised for the greatest number of Rosaries.

The recitation of the Rosary before the Lord Jesus in the Church has very great power. The Rosary before the Blessed Sacrament has inconceivable power of intercession.

The Mother Most Holy desired from the children in Fatima a dependable integrity, and these children truly did penance, truly made sacrifices, truly brought in a great contribution of Rosaries. They accomplished all this, so that we can only adore the Immaculate Heart of Mary whose Motherhood moulded them thus.

We have to put great stress on sacrifices, on mortification, and we should even speak to small children about this, in the same way as we speak to adults, and to live this. It is especially necessary to remember this: *"All power is given to Me in Heaven and on earth"*, and to remember about this, so that people would know that the Lord Jesus has in His Own hands that which they will do, and they should offer sacrifices and appeasement through the Heart of Mary.

62.   The Lord Jesus said: *"Into Your hands I commend My Spirit."*

All of your life is a preparation for this; to have the power at the moment of death to say this which the Lord Jesus said: *"Father, into Your Hands I commend my spirit."*

The condition of this is that the entire life, every day, would be united with God through the desire of offering it as the greatest glory to God. The prescription for this will be an absolute ceasing of self-seeking. In this there will be the sign of a certain self-control; whether one is doing this for God, because it is the Will of God. Then in like mind one accepts a blessing on one's matters, and also on the seeming non-attainment of the goal. The bestowal of Divine value on one's own affairs, on one's own action and on one's own words – all have to be in the area of personal action. The seeking of an immediate sign (for example, the hearing of a prayer) is petty-minded and is a denial of the slogan "Jesus I trust in You".

The purpose of the human being is the giving of glory to God, and this is easily, lightly and simply achieved when it is united with me, and is in accordance with my maternal teachings and examples which are set aside for the children in the Rosary. For example, two identical sources: the first confers supernatural value to his action, and the second does not, and no one from outside can force this on him. The source does not succeed, but if he had done this for God the aim would have been achieved. In this there is great prodigality.

The SECRET POWER of the ROSARY

63.   The Rosary is complete. Everything is in it. Love is everything. God is Love. With the lens one gathers the rays of love and graces, and through the Rosary they are directed to where the Heart of the Mother of God is, in which all the rays of love and grace are concentrated, and through her they are directed to where they are very, very, necessary. Happy are those who live in the brightness of these rays, and in proximity to this Heart, in the warmth and safety of maternal love. The rays from the lens reach out so far and are so strong that they burn evil, so that with the Rosary in the hand and in the mouth, with a humble heart and with trust, let you expect a measure beyond that which your poor tiny heads and hearts can conceive and feel.

Let you be like little children. They say the Rosary in the family, because Mama bade them, and they do not at all worry about what will be the outcome of this. Such trust, such confidence beats back all superfluous worries, so how would they be obliged! Be mindful about the Mother Most Holy and how much she means to you... We are helping you in this, only there must, of necessity, be visible, audible and spiritual unity, i.e. the Rosary said and united in spirit with the Mother Most Holy in the individual mysteries.

64.   Let you meditate on the Divine Love in the Rosary.

Of all things love is the most perfect. The Lord Jesus brought a fire on earth, and wished only this – that hearts would burn with love. The Rosary is a twofold gift of love. The first gift is found in what it contains, and the second in the mould given to the people. The Rosary contains an unending gift of Divine Love for those who accept it with love. "You will be drawing out with joy from the well of the Saviour." The Rosary is literally, this vessel for drawing out, and the Mother Most Holy is, as it were, pouring out into this vessel.

The Mother of God wishes that the Rosary would be loved. The Mother Most Holy, so expressively and so many times, revealed her will in the matter of the Rosary, that here there is no longer anything to be philosophised. As Queen, she demonstrated the power of the Rosary in all peoples, and in all trials, so that here there is no longer anything to doubt, to prove, to seek. Each of the mysteries is a gift, with the power to completely absorb the heart and the mind. *It is necessary to say the Rosary every day.*

The Heart of the Mother of God is the pleasing dwelling place of the entire Most Holy Trinity. With each mystery, with concentration, to consider and to enter in spirit into the Most Sweet Heart of the Mother of God, and in it to glorify the Most Holy Trinity, and to unite oneself with God through it – is a well-said Rosary.

65. Immediately after the Resurrection of Christ the Lord and after leaving the garden, the women and the Apostles together with the Mother Most Holy started the cult of the Most Holy Face of the Lord Jesus. It is very necessary that we should take care that our faces would not be very displeasing to the Most Holy Face. In order to do this it is necessary to know what was expressed on the Holy Face of the Lord Jesus. This was the Face of The God – Man. God is Love. These are the words of Holy Scripture, and the Lord Jesus desired from people love of God and of each other, and not of self and all the Order, founded on love.

The Mother of God did not demand adoration of these two images of faces, which the Lord Jesus left on St. Veronica's and St. Calun's kerchiefs, but she was very pleased and lived with an awareness of this adoration. Already in the mysteries of The Annunciation and The Visitation The Mother of God knew that her Child is God and Saviour, and she was completely thrilled and seized with the desire of seeing and adoring The Face of the Divine Child, in the deepest humility, feeling herself unworthy of this.

In the third mystery the Mother Most Holy first gave the homage of faith, worship and love to the Most Holy Face of the Child, and it was of such, and to such, a degree that she enraptured Heaven and all the Angels, and St. Joseph worshipped the Divine Face of the Child with such annihilation and humility that it is not possible to describe.

In the Presentation and the Finding there is the exhibition of the Face of The Divine Child. Other people looked on this Face, but It (His Divine Majesty) was concealed from them.

It is necessary, in like means, to pass through the life of the Lord Jesus.

Later, from the beginning of the sixth mystery as it was then and as it continues to be (because this endures) we see the part of the Most Holy Face in the work of Redemption. In the entirety of the work of Redemption were the desires of the Father and the tears and bloody sweat of This

Face, and the terrible pain reflected on It: cheeks so horribly swollen, spittle so abominable … So, in the Rosary it is necessary to experience each mystery with the Most Holy Virgin Mary, meditating on the mysteries of the Divine Face of the Saviour.

The Glorious mysteries: The Mother of God sees her own Son, but how is she seeing Him and what is this Face like – after the Resurrection?

The Ascension: The eyes of everyone were fixed on the Holy Face, which moved away, but yet it remains. The Assumption: The Mother of God so very much desired this, that we are not able to comprehend it. The Coronation: Not seeing, not knowing, we adore the Most Holy Face of the Lord Jesus crowning His Own Mother, and we adore her Royal Maternal Face immersed in adoration loving the Most Holy Face of her Son to a degree of which no one, either of Angels or Saints is capable.

66. The Rosary is the great holy word. It is the great holy weapon and the great holy act. Each Rosary, which is well said, is the great holy victory, which endures, and will endure, forever. The Rosary must reign in the entire spiritual life of every person. Such is its destiny, and such is the Will of Heaven. He who proclaims the glory of the Rosary has special graces to do this and also for carrying it out. The Rosary must have apostles assigned solely to do this. The Rosary forms great characters. The Rosary gives a true and genuine joining together of all the people who are saying it, even though they are not acquainted, and do not know about this.

The SECRET POWER of the ROSARY

The saying of the Rosary is the taking and the using of this weapon, which is to carry the victory. Since the Commander says that one has to use this weapon, it is not possible to take another – even though it would be the best.

Through faith in the power of the Rosary we receive its power. It is possible, before a given mystery, to say "I desire through the power of this mystery ..." or "I call on the power of this mystery for the intention..."

One means of saying the Rosary is to gaze, as the power of God in a given mystery hides, reveals, and acts.

The power of God in the second part of the Rosary is – in humiliation. If people were to conceive of this there would be given to them this solution: this means that a greater faith would be developed in the Divine power which hides itself, reveals itself and acts in the Rosary. And this power has to give peace! Peace now, and peace in the face of whatever will be. Divine action is only in peace, and this peace, in order that it would be under Divine action, it is necessary to struggle for it through the Rosary. Peace is a gift of the Lord Jesus, but it is necessary to reach for peace, to get it, to hold it and to distribute it, and to achieve all this through the Rosary. When one proclaims a sermon it is possible, and necessary, to tie in each thing with one of the fifteen mysteries of the Rosary – even to extend it – and then many of the resistances of the people against the Rosary disappear. The Rosary will flow like a river.

67. All the mysteries of the Rosary – is a struggle. For so very long in the Church there was tolerated the spirit of light sentimentality, of empty phrases, and effacing of limits. This is disobedience to the Will of God, which the Most Holy Mother and the Popes revealed.

Many times it is heard in the world: "Such a spirit of utilisation has prevailed now." Such in itself is a stock-phrase, and does not take seriously the contents of each word:

That spirit, truly,
that prevails;
that utilisation, truly.

In each of the mysteries of the Rosary there is a struggle. This is a direct struggle with satan, in which he is threatened with the weapon of the Rosary, which is the devastation of his activity, and also the treatment of the wounds of this fight. The entire strategy, which is the planning of this fight, which has assured victory, exists.

The first mystery struggles against the rebellion of the angels – against the first rebellion of creatures:

non serviam – ecce Ancilla;
pride – annihilation in humility;
contempt – acceptance, with the greatest and the highest love;
the throwing down into the gulf – the elevation, "He Who is Mighty has done great things for me."

Likewise, it is possible to specify different thoughts, such as those given here, in each individual mystery.

68 Fatima is the turning point in the history of mankind. This signpost was given on earth, and whoever, glancing to Heaven, sees it, must undertake a decision, just like every person standing before a signpost. This signpost says: "Here is the gulf of fire – there is Heaven." Wishing to avoid the gulf – you must strive for Heaven.

All the mysteries of the Rosary form one whole: the life of Jesus in Mary, the life of Mary in God the Holy Trinity, and the lives of Jesus and Mary in us. As in the entire Rosary all Heaven is involved – Angels and Saints – so also, in order to direct the people from the different unbeaten tracks at this turning where the signpost stands, the Angels and Saints are taking part. This decision is then taken with the participation of all Heaven.

When we are saying the Rosary we turn our attention to those elect in Heaven who are particularly connected with the given mystery.

The Annunciation – the Archangel Gabriel.

The Visitation – St. Joseph, Zachary and his wife Elizabeth, and St. John in the womb of his Mother.

Let us love them and have a particular devotion to them, remembering about the Angels of this mystery, and they will be helping us so that these mysteries would be in us, and we in them.

In the Nativity – the Angel who wakened the shepherds, uncountable hosts of Angels who are singing glory to God, and proclaiming peace to the people.

The shepherds – these were real saints, chosen, privileged, chaste, simple souls.

Shepherds of Bethlehem pray for us and for our parish.

The Three Kings – these are real saints worthy of admiration and imitation, and God in them is adored.

Three Holy Kings pray that all humanity would seek the truth that all nations would come and bow to the King, for which everything lives. Come let us bow!

Let us examine in thought, and let us draw near in heart to those who are in each mystery. We are meditating on how very pleasing they are to God, how they are chosen through Providence – just these and not others! – how their pure and simple hearts became more pure and filled with God and with these Holy Mysteries. Such is the wisdom and mercy of God that for us, in some of the mysteries, He abolishes the border covering the activity and life of the Angels, how the Angels are drawing near to the Saints, and the Saints, already in this life, are uniting with the Angels. Let us take the persons of Simeon and Anna. His Lord God chose, and destined, that Simeon would take the Child in his hands and sing the hymn, which, to the end of the world, will come from countless hearts raised to God.

St. Simeon, pray for us.

St. Anna, the model of service to God, in prayer, fasting, in mortification, and in good works, ask for us this grace, that God would deign to call many women on this way, because the Church needs their activity very much.

Her character is to represent a model and consolation to those despised by the world "to the stupid of the world" who often mock piety, although respect is due to praying, simple souls. Satan would very much like to twist it, and it is necessary to look after them.

In the fifth mystery we have those who were heartily perturbed by the pain of Mary and Joseph and they wished to help. There were those who looked on this with an evil eye, and in their hearts they felt evil. There were, among the priests, those who, in amazement, sensed the Divine Word and the Divine action, and who, knowing their own misery, - perhaps not as much as they ought, although they had the feeling of their own sins – considered: "perhaps this has already happened; perhaps the expectation has been fulfilled." And also they felt that they were unworthy, and that this would be too simple. Their hearts stirred, but the stand of others overpowered and stifled them. This mystery endures through eighteen years of the Hidden Life of the Lord Jesus.

Here, for adoration, for imitation, and for loving, are the Most Holy Ones of all, as they were, are, and will be – The Holy Family: God – the Son, Mary – the Mother, and humble St. Joseph.

69.   The Assumption of the Mother of God.

O Mary conceived without sin, pray for us who have recourse to Thee.

The privilege of the Mother of God of being conceived without sin, became the entitlement of her Assumption. The Mother of God sometimes appears on earth, and
- gives her decrees,
- dispenses privileges,
- warns,
- reprimands,
- bestows,
- encourages,
- rescues,

and in all this she loves everyone.

Through these revelations she gives to us the possibility of becoming more and more acquainted with her own action. She shows the full mercy of God, and more and more of the bright and powerful eternal truths stand before the eyes. Therefore, the acceptance of these revelations, dissemination of them, listening to them, and co-operation with them, and the matters therein, is such a burning desire of her Heart. Such a joy of her Heart it would be if her children were to receive it, and His Heart would confer on their children a great reward.

And therefore, in these things there is nothing tri-fling, nothing which would be possible to disregard, and there is nothing, which if disregarded, would not be enor-mous in its consequences.

And here lies the whole reason why, that for all eter-nity they have significance; such small facts as acceptance or non-acceptance of the leaflet (on which is written the desires of the Blessed Mother, in Fatima), the pressing to the heart, or, the despising of the Medal; the kiss of the dy-ing lips on the Scapular, or, the tearing off of it before death.

O Mary conceived without sin, gloriously assumed, crushing the head of satan with your foot, pouring a con-tinuous stream of graces on all humanity on the globe of the earth, time after time coming down to the earth from Heaven, transforming the world into your Son's and your own Kingdom, and rescuing souls for your own Son for eternity. Queen of Heaven and of us, reign over us, com-mand us, reprimand us. Most Merciful, watch over us, save us, and pull us away from the slavery of satan, because we are calling to you: "O Mary conceived without sin, pray for us who have recourse to Thee."

The SECRET POWER of the ROSARY

May you receive from us this call: O Mary conceived without sin, pray for us who have recourse to Thee, and for those who do not have recourse to Thee, and may you reign over us on earth here, and in eternity in Heaven – Queen of the Universe, Queen of Paradise, Queen forever. Amen.

70. I m there where they need me. I am there where they are calling to me, and I am there where they are not calling, and where, in their erroneous opinion, they do not need me. I am there to prevent ruin, *subvenire ruinae.* Every king on earth is dependent on having the most subjects. I also desire to have the most. My way is easy, direct and unfailing.

To refuse the Queen when she asks for a levy is to lose grace with her. But this refers to earthly queens. And when few are giving to me, I am looking to see if there will not be an overweight from one side, so that the general balance would be such, that with my Son The King I could – with contributions on the weight of the treasure for equalising the debt of the world – be able to support my requests for the world.

Do you think that I am getting it? This treasure – this surplus?

Satan approaches, woe!

You have the unending merits of my Son, His Incarnation – through all His earthly life – to the triumph of the Ascension, and to the triumph of life in souls. This is contained in the Rosary, and only this has worth.

You have the devotion to Mercy, although you do

not wish to entreat earnestly with it. (Resistance to the confirmation of the Divine Mercy and to acceptance of it).

There are lonely Queens, widowed and such who have awaited exile. This, which is going on, answers this description: In the laments of Jeremiah you find a description of this, which is and which has to be. Let you sympathise with the sorrows of my Heart which is united with the agony of my Son; you are seeing the non-utilisation of the Most Holy Sacrifice for many, many souls. Let your hearts be more concentrated. Let you seek with ardent hearts to make sacrifices. For temptations of superfluity, of inefficacy, let you make acts of trust.

71.   The tenth mystery of the Holy Rosary – Jesus died.

I was His Mother from the moment of conception in Nazareth to Golgotha, to the laying of Him in the grave, and I am She forever.

Thanks to this I became, and I am, Mother of all who are brought forth – throughout their lives as well as at their dying – and I desire to be their Mother for eternity.

The pain of my Immaculate Heart – is caused by the temporal death of many on account of sins, and by the eternal death of many. I am repeating: "Make sacrifices to me in order to save them."

The eleventh mystery of the Holy Rosary: I am the Mother of the Resurrected Jesus. Through this I became, and I am, Mother of all those who at the judgement will become resurrected to eternal life, and I am the Mother of those who, accepting the grace of loving repentance through penance, are resurrecting to new life. I am declaring this to you today, because my Son wishes that I would be more known and loved, not only through knowledge and theology, but also through the hearts of the people. I am with those who are weeping and are burying their dead, and with those who, after the victory through humiliation and pain, are resurrecting. I am with you always.

The Angels at the empty grave: When you die to yourselves, through the death of the old person; when on reception of the Lord you are emptying your hearts, I am laying in you, My Son, as I did in the new grave, and He, resurrecting, as He left the Holy Shroud in the grave, likewise in your soul He leaves a likeness of Himself and places a guard of Holy Angels in it.

The glory of the Resurrection came into being from pain, humiliations, and the surrendering of self to the Will of the Father in love. With you it is the same: Let you not worry then about the time of the resurrection and its glory – let you maintain humility, let you love the Will of God, and in your suffering let you possess your souls. Through the Resurrection of the Son, I became Mother and Virgin of the Most Holy Sacrament – let you bend your steps with me there, because there, is the entire Jesus: in swaddling clothes and a crown of thorns, in the weakness of an infant and in the weakness of the agony of death, and all this became the triumph of the victory. Then, let you rejoice and be glad always and in everything, praying unceasingly, with thanksgiving. One Fiat in the acceptance of a new cross and one act of love in tears – is the glory of God, which testifies to satan that the world is not his, because such souls exist … such souls exist, always.

Your great desire of holiness, of drawing near to

God and uniting with Him here and forever – this is my joy and this gives consolation to my Heart.

72. "I am the field flower and the lily of the valley." If you were to know the beauty, majesty and glory, the power, the rule and the kindness of the Queen! Heaven is full of the majesty of her glory – earth has also to be full, and to achieve this Rosaries, which are the crown of her glory, and with which the inhabitants of earth are crowning her, are a necessity.

What would the earth be without Rosaries, which are continually going from the thoughts, hearts and lips of the people? You do not know, and you cannot conceive of this. How short is the time of life in the face of eternity, and how short is the time set aside in life for the weaving of Crowns of Rosaries for our and your Queen!

Some of the Saints had unveiled only the border of her Queenly glory, which was as much as they were able to endure. It is possible to be completely peaceful, knowing that the Most Holy Mother, as Queen of the Universe, conducts order, marshals everything, spreads her own people in appropriate positions, purifies, destroys every evil, sets her own angelic guards wherever they are necessary, enlightens and strengthens in the hearts of the people the Law of God, pours out on each and every one, and on everything, an abundance of graces, reaps them to herself and offers them to her Son, the King, and with her own triumphing Immaculate Heart pays the deepest, and most perfect homage of love and devotion: "Behold, My Son, purified and prepared through me, those people of the world which you gave to me. – Reign!"

In order to hasten, to purify, and to act with and for Mary, The Queen, so that the Kingdom and the Triumph of Both Most Holy Hearts would come, you can act, and you have to act, through the Rosary, the holiness, the importance and the power of which was uncovered and shown to you.

Let you trust, and let you act, and may no one be lost in this fight. May no one who is united with Mary through the Rosary be lost. In the Rosary, as in a mirror, one sees the model of the virtues of Mary, Queen of the Rosary, and utilises graces therefrom to repair and to sanctify life according to her pattern, and, in obedience, believes, trusts and loves. Such a one conquers, because his Queen is the Victorious Rosary Queen. Likewise, the Carmelite Scapular also gives its privilege, which is the seal of her promise of a happy death and of birth into Heaven. Amen.

73.   The Twelfth Mystery, The Ascension. This is something we ought to have continuously in mind, in heart, in thanksgiving and in desire. For the reason that if one does not think about Heaven, and if one does not have this purpose continuously and distinctly before one's eyes in everything, then one easily accepts the swindle of satan, such as the expression "heaven on earth".

But the more one removes oneself from the earth and everything that is of the earth, the nearer one is to the genuine Heaven, and this Heaven comes about here on earth through those who are most torn away from the earth, and most united with Heaven, i.e. the Saints. The earth is the terrain of the battle of hell against Heaven, the battle that began from the rebellion of the Angels, and which endures continually, but its terrain is only on the earth. The earth, however, has all the makings of the genuine vestibule of Heaven, as it is for the chosen ones or the Saints, who, "amid the volatility of this world, persist in peace".

And that which persists is that which is in peace, and it is already part of Heaven, because it is, as it were, drawn out from this Divine persistence. And God is the God of Peace, and in peace, lives. God acts there where there is peace. There has to be endurance in peace, in the intense making of one's way towards the mystery of the Ascension.

With the grace and prize of this precise mystery is the understanding that
- I either win Heaven, or I lose it,
- I either draw near to it, or I remove from it,
- I either embellish it, or I diminish its glory with my own person,
- I am either opening Heaven to others and I am bringing them to Heaven, or I am not doing this, although this is my duty, and I am removing others from Heaven and pushing them into the pit.

And this is what one does in every moment of life and in every matter. This is most important to the understanding. (This is all very simple. One knows this, only it is necessary to keep it in mind).

Conclusion: God destined us for Heaven. The Lord Jesus opened Heaven to us, and the Most Holy Mother draws us, helps us, and if such is possible to say, through the Holy Angels she pushes and drives us. But this precipitous path, which was cleared by Lucifer and his own is always open.

Everyone ought to understand and take this to heart that the entrance for each of us to Heaven is the Will of God. If, therefore, one desires to enter Heaven in this way, this desire is purified. There are those who desire Heaven and its happiness without taking the Lord into consideration in it. They would be satisfied with the gifts of God, without God. There are people who know and believe that there is Heaven and there is joy in it for those who desire to do the Will of God, and who desire God in general. They would be satisfied with the gifts of God without God. They are the glow of the awful age. They do not wish to be in Heaven through fulfilment of the Will of God, because they have a hatred of God, and do not wish to have happiness from God. It is very important to know and understand this, because in this is the entire essence of departure, of damnation. And this exists in some people, even in the attitudes of people – "I know that what you are giving me is good, but I do not wish to accept it because it is from you." Where your treasure is there also is your heart. As one desires God, so one desires Heaven. Our obligation, the fulfilment of which consoles the Immaculate Heart of Mary, is the desire for Heaven, the aspiration to Heaven, the living in Heaven with heavenly thought and heart. This cuts the earthly ties and, in fact, fully helps and leads to Heaven. And all this ought to be finished with the words, which establish the highest law with which one ought to embrace everything – the Will of God! This contains in itself everything. But this is a mystery on which it would be possible to reflect thirty times in a month, and in spite of this, as much knowledge would be drawn out of it, as would be drawn by a bird's beak from the sea.

74. My children, My children, do not fear anything, either now or later. You have the Rosary. You have good will, but it is necessary for you to have an increase in faith, hope and love. *"You of little faith, why did you doubt?"* Inasmuch as there is a lack of faith, there is straight away also a lack of hope and a lack of love: bitterness towards the Lord Jesus. The saying that faith works miracles became mocked and regarded, through the devil, as suggestion. In this way the world reshaped it for something completely different, without this value, which is most essential.

And so it is, not only with this but with other things also. And here it is necessary to recall this: *"Why did you doubt?"* and *"Lord increase our faith"*. It is not possible to say that doubt seized, because this would be to cast off the blame from oneself. If somebody would possess in the will – without regard to doubt – that great certainty flowing from faith he would, through all trials pass on to victory.

The Queen has her own people, her own kingdom. With what terrible pain she looks at the state of her kingdom. Her Son, the King also looks, and does not wish that it would continue thus any longer, but the Mother beseeches that He would not yet make order, and that it is not yet necessary to throw out this or that, and that she will transform it so that it will be of use. And the Son waits. And the Mother Most Holy endeavours to utilise this time in order, still, to rescue. In this work of saving the world, how the Angels and Saints desire to help the Blessed Mother! It is not an exaggeration, that there never was such a time of activity of Angels and Saints as there is now. They desire this because the Mother of God desires it; therefore, all are intent with the desire of rescuing.

Likewise, as the Mother of God is being pleased with Holy Communion of recompense (on the first Saturday of each month), she desires also to have, as the Lord Jesus had, her own Bethany, but these Bethanys have to be in individual homes, families and parishes. It is necessary to encourage people to become a little islet on which the eyes of the Mother and Son will be looking with delight. May there be, among an entire village of drunkards, even one family who would be an example of the children of God, and already this would be like those ten, acquired by haggling, from Sodom and Gomorrah. Let such a family say to itself: "We wish to be such a Bethany." And if it is not possible for all the family to do this – even a few persons, or even one, may focus as a lens radiating glances of the love of the Mother and Son.

It is necessary to direct the will of the people towards sacrifices for the Blessed Mother.

When a purpose is set each one finds a means, because in the will of these people there is a field for the action of the Holy Spirit in order to give such little centres where there would be the beginning of the kingdom of Mary. Pictorially it is possible to present it thus: When the heads of a district are giving an account that here there was a flood, and there a fire, and then one of them tells, that here remained unharmed. Then the Queen replies that "Fortunately, it was not harmed."

The Mother of God of the Miraculous Medal pours graces on all her own little kingdoms, and later takes the whole world and offers it to God. This is what Mary, the Queen, wishes: that she would be able to offer each soul to the Most Holy Trinity, as her own kingdom, and in the greatest humility to say: "I have conquered."

As one says the Rosary carefully and piously – "Thy Kingdom come"… and these Hail Marys… - it is by this means that one opens the kingdom, builds, encompasses and closes it.

75. To day let there be a word about the Church being brought forth in the thirteenth mystery. We have to meditate according to the usual methods:

The Apostles:

1. Where? In the Cenacle, which was locked for fear of the Jews.

2. When? After their Lord and Master removed Himself to Heaven, when they felt uncertain, fearful, and abandoned. But still they did not comprehend everything; they still did not have understanding, but only some indistinct intuition in hearts already consoled, and through separation and longing, already perplexed.

3. In what was it? In what did their most important act reveal itself? In obedience and perseverance, which was without any limitation. It is necessary to pay attention to this. There are people who reckon thus: "For three days we have been praying, well, and what?" "For six days we have been praying, well, and what?" And they trusted and were

prepared to pray for 99 days. All their own distress, long-ing, uncertainty, desires, and such tormenting confusion with words, which were completely interior, they deposited at the feet of the Mother Most Holy. She took them and gave them the glow of her own Heart, in order that their hearts would be enflamed in Him. She gave them a share in her own merits in this mystery. This means that all this, which they obtained as recompense for their service, such as

- the obedience of returning to Jerusalem,
- the will to persevere,
- endurance,
- and prayer. All this flowed on them from Mary.

But the condition was this: that these small, poor people would deposit at her feet everything that they pos-sessed. Already, immediately after the Passion of the Lord Jesus they orientated themselves properly, as they sensed what the Mother of God has to be.

Ashamed and humiliated they looked, as it were, with a certain jealousy on Saint John, who was so clearly privileged. They understood that Saint John, because of what he had done, received the privilege of Sonship – and they also wished, but lacked the courage, to do something in order that they would have a share in this.

Behold, how people after a mishap, have to come back.

If they had not united with the prayers of the Blessed Mother, their prayers alone would not have drawn down, so easily, the Holy Spirit. (Analogy between the first and thirteenth mysteries, because the prayer of the Blessed Mother draws, hastens, and brings the action and the sending of the Holy Spirit. Only that there the Mother of God is alone, in secret, and here she is in the circle of the Apostles).

In what has been said up to now, each one who meditates finds for himself, and will know how to draw out, instruction for meditation. The people praying at the feet of Mary, and waiting for the sending down of the Holy Spirit and the renewal of the face of the earth are now, also, only a handful in comparison with all the ocean of enemies, atheists, those seduced in heresies, pagans, and the indifferent. This meditation of today is for this: that we would know and speak about it with others, that it is not necessary to count three days or six days, because for certain there will come such a day. And for us it is necessary to deposit at the feet of the Mother of God that which they deposited, and perhaps to imitate one of them; maybe Saint John in his faith and love, peace and courage, or, those ten other Apostles – in their contrition and humility, in hope and entreaty, in thanksgiving and annihilation, but everything – in the purity of a free heart, so that the Holy Spirit can deposit there the embers of His Fire.

The Mother of God in Fatima set out certain desires. These are the means of the Mother Most Holy, which the Church has to renew and regenerate. Here we have these same themes of obedience, of following after Mary and of persevering with her: she promised and that is all. It is necessary to imitate Saint John or the ten Apostles. Such is the means picked by the Mother Most Holy for those who wish Her to pour out the Holy Spirit on the world.

The SECRET POWER of the ROSARY

76.   The purpose of a person on earth is the giving of glory to God through fulfilment of the Will of God – and his final goal is Heaven. This is the return to the Father – told by the Lord Jesus at the Ascension; and in the Father's house there are many mansions. But everything is penetrated and embraced with love.

It is necessary to remember in every moment of life, in all our affairs, joys, sufferings and work to unite with the Lord God through Mary. The Mother Most Holy demands this, desires this, and with this directs. The greater the unity the greater is the power in activity, and the greater the happiness the nearer the goal – because Heaven, which is the final goal, is exactly this most perfect unity with the Lord God.

The Mother Most Holy, who directs all this gives us, nothing else – only the Rosary, and the devil, the world and the flesh fights against it. The Rosary gives the victory over the devil, the world and the flesh.

Thanks to what, does the Rosary conquer? Thanks to what has it such power of conquering? It is thanks to this: that into our minds and hearts falls the life of the Lord Jesus most closely united with Mary.

Protestants adore the life of the Lord Jesus, evading His saints, but this is, as it were, a mutilation of the same basis, since with the juices not circulating, it is not possible to expect the holiness of the fruits. This observation of the life of the Lord Jesus and knowledge of Him through the Heart of Mary, and with her, ensures the quickest and the most perfect knowledge of the Lord Jesus and unity with Him.

Meditation on the mysteries is for this: that through

it we would recognise in the life around – in all matters, people, events, and above all in ourselves – the mysteries of the Lord Jesus and Mary: Jesus living in Mary – and Jesus living in us. This leads us quickly to the fullness of the age of Christ.

Hail Mary sets out the quintessence of the first mystery, and in the first mystery everything is contained. The Hail Mary is spread throughout all the mysteries. The Hail Mary is something, which seals each mystery. The Angelic Greeting links us to the work of the Redemption of the world, to the plan of the Father for the Redemption of the world, to the fulfilment of this plan through the Divine Son, and to the activity of the Holy Spirit, from which activity in Mary the Redemption was begun. *"The Holy Spirit will descend upon you, and the power of the most high will overshadow you."*

Everybody must understand that the giving to the world of the Rosary is the Will of God given through Mary. She gave it, and now she reminds us, begs us and commands us to say it. Everybody ought to listen, because in this lies the merits and the beginning of the flow of further graces. It is, as it were, the turning on of a tap, the opening of a spring. As one takes the Rosary in hand, already graces are flowing.

77.   Through the Rosary, one adores the plan of the Father – the carrying into effect of the action of the Redemption of humanity. This began in the first mystery with the great co-operation of the Mother of God, and persists to the fifteenth. If people had kept the Rosary through all the ages, they would never have gone into the heresy of Lutheranism, which despoiled the inclusion of the Mother of God's co-operation in the Redemption, and there would not have been all those heresies, which rejected the Blessed Mother. Instead of glorifying God the Father, and admiring the plan of the Redemption, they mutilated, deformed and corrupted it. Their relation to God the Father and the entire Most Holy Trinity is falsified, because they did not accept this plan in the most essential of its parts.

The saying of the Rosary has to awaken us to the worshipping of God the Father, to loving God the Father, to thanksgiving to God the Father and, through consideration of the relation of the Lord Jesus and Mother of God to the Will of God the Father, it has to teach us devotion to the Will of God.

It is contained in two points: in love and obedience, dependent on vigilant and penetrating knowledge of what the Will of God is. The more we will try to imitate and liken ourselves to the Lord Jesus and His Mother Most Holy, the better we will fulfil the Will of God, because this is what the Lord God desires.

As long as, by means of the Rosary, the effects of heresy is not being extracted from souls, so long will there not be the possibility of cementing humanity into one. The time when there will be one fold and one shepherd will follow when the Rosary chains of all are united, because, only in the Rosary is the entirety of our faith accessible for every one. Let humanity accept the Rosary. And the entire composition of Divine Truths contained in the Rosary, the understanding of them, the acceptance of them to the heart and the will – this let us leave to the action of grace contained in the Rosary. This resolves itself in whether one gives a place to the Mother of God for her activity in the Church and in life, such as God gave her in His Own plan – and not that one gives the Mother of God a certain title and that is all.

78.   Just as the Holy Spirit desires devotion for my veneration, and it gladdens Him, so also, I desire that hearts would burn with particular love, and that there would bloom a particular devotion to the Holy Spirit. Let you take what Holy Scripture says about the Holy Spirit, or what the Holy Spirit says about Himself. *"Those who are ruled by the Holy Spirit are those who are the sons of God." "He will teach you the whole truth."* Without the activity of the Holy Spirit you know nothing, you are acquainted with nothing, and you will do nothing. Acquaintance with my Son comes as a result of prayer to the Holy Spirit. The world has to know my Son, and to answer His call and invitation: *"Come follow Me."* Rosary devotion has to awaken and renew devotion to the Holy Spirit. Let Veni Creator, Veni Sancte, and antiphons, which interlace in the liturgical year, grow to become daily prayers. It is necessary to reflect, in the deepest humility, on the deepest mysteries of the Most Holy Trinity. There is never too long an expectation as a result of calling on the Holy Spirit. The characteristic of the action of the Holy Spirit is urgency, and as a result – everything changes. The power of His action is in darkness, sweetness, and in poverty, with full virtue and spiritual offering, and with the result of triumph in brightness, happiness, and peace, because where the Holy Spirit is, there the spirits of darkness take flight. Thus it has to be for the world, and all this has to happen through Mary.

As it is not possible to set apart devotion to the Lord Jesus from the Mother Most Holy in any of the mysteries, likewise, it is not possible to conceive of devotion to the Holy Spirit without the co-operation of the Mother Most Holy; without her humility and perseverance in prayer.

In saying the Rosary it is not possible to disregard any of the mysteries – and for to day I am giving a reminder and a sweet command, in order that the 13th mystery would be said, as it ought to be said. Doing this, we come to know the activity, help and love of the Sweetest Heart of the most humble Mary. And still one more enlightenment: the Holy Spirit burns, purifies and changes everything else, only it is necessary, through humility, to make a place for His activity. Nothing prevents the activity of the Holy Spirit, no misery, only there must be humility. If this is not present, the doors remain closed.

79.　　The Mother Most Holy is the most perfect of creatures, which came from the Hands of God. It is necessary to remember about this and often to return to it in thought. It is well to turn to the Lord God and the Mother Most Holy personally in thought. What when people do not have in thought and in heart this adoration, this respect for the greatness and power of the Mother Most Holy? This is commonplace. In the Rosary, through saying it with reverence, we have to make recompense for this, so that many of us poor people can endure. This ought not in the least degree to impede us from direct approach to the Mother of God. It is only necessary to remember Her Majesty, dignity, her fullness of virtue and grace, to pay homage to the Mother of God, and with her, to thank the Lord God in each mystery of the Rosary for this.

It suffices to consider with what kind of reverence the Archangel Gabriel spoke to the Mother of God about conceiving the Son of God. In the third mystery the Kings truly gave homage, and with complete ceremony, they expressed the highest feelings, which to God are due. It is necessary to proceed thus in all of the mysteries of the Rosary, and only this will be pleasing to the Mother Most Holy and to the Lord Jesus. Such recitation will be compensation for our sins and the sins of others in this regard.

80.   The fact that the Rosary is so despised or neglected, or so modified, or plainly derided, combated, and so often mangled and trampled upon, that even through those who have been saying it often, have said it neglectfully and finally shoved it away, in a word through the believers and the non-believers the Rosary being regarded as nothing, or as something very insignificant – demonstrates its greatness, importance and power.

All devotion to the Mother of Sorrows is included in the Rosary. Whether it be the grief of the Mother Most Holy at the flight into Egypt, or the shedding of the Blood of the Lord Jesus at the circumcision – all is found there included in the Rosary when one embraces, with thought and heart, the width and depth of the mysteries of the Rosary.

In saying the Rosary it is possible before each of the sorrowful mysteries to recall a certain verse from the Sequence about the Sorrowful Mother of God (Stabat Mater).

In such saying of the Rosary there will be devotion to the Mother of Sorrows, to Her Immaculate Heart pierced with the Sword of Sorrow, to the Passion, to the Precious Blood and to the Most Sacred Heart of the Lord Jesus. For many people this simplifies, teaches, enlightens and deepens their prayer and meditation. They become acquainted with finding out about the greatness, importance, holiness and power of the Holy Rosary. And God in the Unity of the Most Holy Trinity will be adored in the Word Incarnate, through Whom was brought about your salvation; and everything in Mary, with Mary, through Mary and for Mary. Amen.

81. I am with you and in you when my Son is living in you. My heart is together with His Most Sacred Heart on the Miraculous Medal: The Cross of His Sacrifice grows from the letter of my name; from my offering, which the Father desired and the Son deigned to accept. Since the Fiat in the first mystery our Hearts are beating in one rhythm, together adoring, together loving, together saving together suffering, together thanking, excusing, recompensing, together giving satisfaction, together triumphing, together desiring the hearts of all humanity, in order to unite them with Ours, with this same rhythm beating, this same action, because this is their salvation, and their way to it.

There is an invocation: *"Heart of Mary most closely united with the Heart of Jesus, pray for us."* This prays for the drawing of your hearts to Our Hearts, and for the uniting of your hearts with Ours. It is very necessary to watch over the purity of your hearts; to be anxious about this, so that every movement of your human hearts would be able to unite to Our Hearts! How seed of all kinds, and all kinds of pollen sown by the enemy in your hearts, saddens Our Hearts! The Holy Spirit says: "With a humble contrite spirit, God will not despise you." When a sinner ponders the torment of Our Hearts in the sorrowful mysteries let him show good will. Then through the merits of this torment, the spirit of repentance and penance descends upon him.

When praying for sinners it is necessary in all the mysteries, successively, to offer to the Eternal Father the merits of Our Hearts; appealing to Their Love. With this one hastens the arrival of the time of the visible triumph of Our Hearts, with which will triumph the hearts of all the chosen ones.

82. In the first mystery of the Rosary the Mother of God said "Fiat" for this: that She would conceive and bear a Son, and then everything else, in addition, was given to her. There was no reckoning that she would become Queen of Martyrs and so on, but in this Fiat there was agreement to each desire of God. The Mother of God would have made the same reply if the Archangel Gabriel had said that she would be the Queen of Martyrs...

When one says "Fiat" to the Will of God then a multitude of things are given, and it is not necessary to count them, and it is exactly this that establishes for us the very important meaning of the first mystery; e.g. suffering comes, and when with deep reverence we give it our fiat, in reward for this there comes, in its own time, disclosure and recognition of this mystery, and an abridgement of the same suffering as well as the appearance of the fruits of this suffering, as they are yielded in us and in our neighbours all around.

83.   In the Rosary there is everything. The Rosary – it is I. I desire good Rosaries because they are my glory, my particular joy in Heaven. It is possible to treat the Rosary as follows:

1.   Three parts as a whole.
2.   A part as a whole.
3.   A decade as a whole.
4.   But also a Hail Mary as a whole, because the Hail Mary is sufficient for meditation on the first mystery.

There is no other greeting to further mysteries, and for them this greeting is appropriate. Therefore, it follows that this mystery embraces the others, and also constitutes the throne around which they arrange themselves. It is like a crystal axle for them. The essence of the first mystery stretches out to all fifteen; in other words to the entire Redemption.

The Rosary is received with reluctance compared to other devotions, because it is so simple. Therefore, they often despise it or raise up a multitude of doubts.

The Rosary has to be said continually, because by doing this there is the continual application of the Works of Redemption contained in the power of the given mystery.

"HAIL MARY, FULL OF GRACE, THE LORD

IS WITH THEE" .... Thus spoke the Archangel Gabriel. This greeting endures. Because once said, it endures. Through the Angelic Greeting we harness ourselves in the Will of God, and in this most essential and most perfect prayer, and in the Divine Will accomplished by the Archangel Gabriel, we also become participants of his merits: obedience to the Father – humility in the presence of the Most Holy Virgin Mary, and also his happiness. He, of all the most perfect of creatures, was acquainted with the Most Holy Virgin Mary – and we through the Rosary, get to know Mary and, in her spirit, all her causes.

After the fulfilment of this mission, the Archangel Gabriel received a higher rank, like a mark of distinction, and this establishes for him happiness beyond degree, which does not grow dim, because it is what it is, solely a mark of distinction, which is entirely in him, and is the object of the joy of all the Angels. And through all the Guardian Angels (and here we are calling them 'Guardians', which means also Angels who guide and govern all things and are, as it were, the Guardian Angels of all these things) all creation together with the Archangel Gabriel is united in this. This is what we are saying to you: The unceasing Hail Marys flowing from your hearts and your lips, unite us with you and are the condition of victory. This is because the Archangel Gabriel was on a mission from the entire Most Holy Trinity, and this mission made the way for the Redemption of all humanity. Therefore, and as a consequence, we are drawn into unity with the Most Holy Trinity and to the co-redeeming of the Most Holy Virgin Mary ... Even thoughtless recitation of the Hail Mary ... has its own power of enlightenment of that which, above, was declared.

84. The Ascension and the Assumption – through the merits of the Mother and Son in these two mysteries to win glory for Heaven! These two mysteries teach us that nothing should discourage us; only to live in the hope of death and the hope of victory in death, and that we should pray very much that for us death would become a triumph.

The Mother of God wishes that those who are already saying the Rosary would be different from those who are not saying it.

People are not thinking about death, and therefore, when it comes, it becomes for them something awful. About these things there is a battle in our souls. Satan cannot bring down childhood; this humiliates him, because he is the spirit of pride. Therefore, all internal struggles are easy when one has the spirit of childhood, because then the Mother of God fights for her child: "What do you desire of him – after all, he is very tiny?"

Satan strikes at the Assumption. The Pope declared this dogma, because faith in this mystery is the key to the opening of the happiness, which does not abandon people in the greatest of sufferings. St. John Bosco began the day with his children with the saying of the Glorious Mysteries.

Satan on the one hand, denies the existence of hell and damnation, under the mask of the goodness of God – fraud. On the other hand, if it is about Heaven, this oozes with the uncertainty as to how this can be. Here is the "uncertainty" that "hell does not exist" and here the "certainty" as to "how can there be Heaven", and so humanity at present is pressed into materialism. He wishes to tear away faith in the existence of hell-fire, and he has led also to the situation where people do not know about the heavenly fire (love) about which they ought to pray, continuously.

There are Angels of the Ascension, and there are Angels of the Assumption. The former and the latter have manifested their presence to people. With the saying of the Rosary, one returns to the Angels of these mysteries.

The Mother Most Holy many a time chooses paupers for action. She is sad when one forgets the form of action is not only in the greatness of the cause, which we are handling, but also in the contribution of suffering. Then what happens is, that this suffering is changed into the joy of which the martyrs, who are seeing Heaven open, are the evidence.

Suffering is not for suffering; it is for nothing else, - only Heaven. Let us try to consider what from today's day, we will find in Heaven; what will I take to Heaven? I cannot take sin, but it is possible to take sorrow.

The Ascension and the Assumption – are the present signposts for people. These are the lights that guide, and towards which to strive. What then, when all this is filled up with a quantity of superfluous matters?

85.   Each act of trust gladdens my Heart.

Each act of thanksgiving consoles my Heart.

Each offering, my Heart accepts.

Each acceptation and suffering given to me – prayer, work and mortification – I hoard.

Each one of you entering on this road is my victory.

And in all this there has to be love, which is the

only payment you have to make for the love of my Heart. There has to be the intention, because the will decides about everything. And above all there has to be acquaintance and acknowledgement of your own misery and complete poverty, because only the poor yield, and only they are pleasing.

And if there is not a place of readiness for my gifts, through poverty, these gifts flowing from my Heart cannot be either directed or joyfully received there. The Rosary has to be this, which prepares your hearts, cleanses and empties them through the clearing out of self-love. The Rosary begs for gifts, prepares gifts and brings gifts, and therefore, life lived with a good, humble, faithful, and loving saying of the Holy Rosary, daily, even though it would be most inconspicuous, and apparently without significance, is not wasted. The value of it will be shown at death and in the life to come.

86.   Just as you are waiting all day for this moment of meditation, so I also am looking forward to it. Each day, each hour, each moment, brings a new outpouring of graces, and they will abound in your hearts *"Then you will look and you will abound: Your hearts will expand and you will be astounded"* ....

It is pleasing to the Lord when, for each grace, you thank Him personally, because then you are better acquainted with the gifts, and through the gifts, with the Giver. And so it is with the gifts of the Holy Rosary, for which the knowledge of the earthly life does not suffice. In order that my will "would become a loving command for the world, it is necessary that the Pope would love it". (Pope Pius XII at Fatima). In order that his words about me would be extended in the world it is necessary that in different, scattered points on the face of the earth, particular people, and also groups, would love and accept this. Acceptance of the Rosary: there is the commercial acceptance – "I have a commodity to dispose of", and there is the filial acceptance – "I get and I share; I take with love and I give with love." There is a multitude of people who are saying the Rosary as drudgery, but there are also those who love it.

The Mother of God would be able to give other kinds of prayers, to which the same graces would be attached, but she gave the Rosary. The concern here is about faith, trust and obedience. In the Rosary there is a request – something of the kind that was in Paradise. It has this same point: Lucifer has this same stratagem, purpose and action against the Rosary and those who truly accept and say it, as against the first people who were gifted with Paradise. Lucifer knows that he himself will not have it – so he does not wish others to have it. He, himself, would never greet, would not express this greeting, and therefore, hinders those who in their hundreds are saying it. Where the Rosary is, where the Rosary truly is – there, in that place, is persecution and victory.

The saying, most piously, of an entire prayer book will not be so persecuted with temptation as the saying of the Rosary. In the saying of the Rosary one fulfils all the conditions of prayer, which the catechism states: there must be humility, perseverance, confidence ……..

The Two Hearts are in each of the fifteen mysteries,

The SECRET POWER of the ROSARY

and also that which has been mentioned many times already: Their mutual love, love of God the Father and love of people, Their sacrifices, merits and sufferings. My Heart is with the Heart of my Son. This Heart embraces the entire Heart of my Son, and the Sacred Heart of the Lord Jesus is the Divine Heart, and His Love embraces all creation, but above all It embraces the Heart of Mary, the Heart which is to Him the most sweet. And can it be closer united? Pervading – it is at the same time pervaded. This mutual pervading constitutes a mystery.

Because the Sacred Heart of the Lord Jesus is the Divine Heart, therefore it is of the Godhead. Mary is so completely in the Heart of the Son that she fills up this terrible partition between God and people. She fills it so completely that there is no longer a partition between God and humanity. And there, where the Divine Mother is not present, nothing of this partition can be filled.

All this is contained in the mysteries of the Rosary. To the Mother of God is due unceasing and particular glory, unlimited thanksgiving, and aspiration to her acquaintance. St. Louis Marie Grignon de Montfort, in thanksgiving for the Rosary, wrote his book.

In the mystery of the Annunciation we are to thank Mary for the glory, which through the merits of this mystery in union with the Heart of Jesus, she gave to God. Likewise, in the second mystery and in the third mystery, and so on in all of them. We are to thank her also for her successive rendering of glory to God, because we ourselves would never be able to give this glory to the Lord God and we would not be able to fill this abyss. It is necessary to thank the Mother of God, for her mediation between God and us, the mediation for which we are all thankful. Thanksgiving in each mystery pleases the Heart of the Mother of God very much. Such thanksgiving will be a genuine recompense for those who do not give thanks. It is necessary to strongly stress at Holy Communions of recompense – to give thanks for the reception of the Lord Jesus, to give thanks to St. Joseph, and to give thanks to Mary for the bravery of her suffering, for her action in Heaven and on earth. Thus, one gives thanks in Heaven. We are to pray with children in the same way – they will seize this with joy, and with joy their hearts will be filled.

The Divine Heart desires that the Heart of His Mother – which through active denial of acquaintance, neglect, omission, and forfeiture of it by many souls – would be known, and if known, venerated and surrounded with thanksgiving.

87. All of the first part of the Rosary is full of St. Joseph. In the first mystery, upon the Mother of God saying that she does not know a husband, the Archangel announcing that her Conception would be from the Holy Spirit, confirmed the virginity of the Betrothed of the Most Holy Virgin Mary.

In the Visitation we see his protective companionship of the Most Holy Mother. He had there a share in the joy of Her Immaculate Heart, in the outpouring of the graces of the Holy Spirit. Modest and humble, he felt unworthy and silently kept out of the way. That which he comprehended, he accepted; what he did not comprehend this also he adored. This mystery became for him the ful-

The SECRET POWER of the ROSARY

filment of the command, given to him through the Angel, that he should accept his Bride without fear. This put an end to his previous unspeakable suffering. Now, he had joy.

In the third mystery – Oh, what great merits he laid down in the presence of the Most Holy Mary and the Word Incarnate! His worry and pain changed into joy, when, falling with his face to the ground, with Mary he adored the Infant God. Having listened intently to the Angelic singing he saw the result of their action in the bringing in of the Shepherds, and the Three Kings, in the spreading of the joy of the Good News. When, at the present time, the Angels are bringing in sinners to Jesus this brings joy to St. Joseph in Heaven, of which the beginning was in the stable.

In the fourth mystery how great was his joy when Simeon became acquainted with the Infant God. This joy established consolation and reward for the future prolonged pain in the flight, and in the exile among the pagans, where The Holy Family was seen as singularly poor, foreign newcomers, although the pagans also had a dim feeling of the hidden mysteries of the Divinity.

In the fifth mystery, after the faultless loss of the Lord Jesus and the immense pain that followed, there were the long years of the hidden life with the God-Man and Mary, His Mother, which were full of unrevealed mysteries, and Heaven concluded these years without his participation on earth in the last acts of the Redemption. This is what God wished.

His merits and his holiness are so pleasing to God, and the love of God the Father and Mary for him is so great, and the glory and power given to him in Heaven is so magnificent that we finish these, our meditations, with a simple call to people: Come together in your love for St. Joseph with the love of God the Father, with the love of the Sacred Heart of the Saviour, with the love of the Most Holy Heart of Mary, with the love of the Saints, with our Angelic love, and with the love of the just on earth: Let you love St. Joseph!

88. I am the Queen – the Queen of Heaven, the Queen of the Universe, and the Queen of Poland. Poland has to populate Heaven. I have to have faithful on earth and subjects in Heaven. To acknowledge the rule, is to acknowledge obligations; dependence has to be constant for each moment, but levies faithfully given in time, are given forever. And your prayers, sacrifices, promises, acts – what kind are they?

There has to be a conscientiousness about the honour, the right and the great glory of the Queen; in her affairs, to act in compliance with her will; to desire to be her glory, to bring her honour, to expand her State and conquests, to be glad with her, to trust her, to surrender to her, to fight with her and for her, to listen to her, to thank her, to beg her, and above all to love and venerate her with the Love of the Most Sacred Heart of Her Son and the Most Chaste Heart of her Betrothed; to desire to see her, to fulfil her will, to be vigilant for her signal, to expand her compass and her rule over souls, to be prepared to give your life for her, and to be happy from this dependence on her here, and forever. Amen.

89. Christo confixus sum cruci. *I live now, not I, Christ lives in me.* If Christ has to live and dwell in me, I must know – Who this is. This is Love. With love the Lord Jesus took flesh, with love He comes. This is the gift of love from the Father, and the same Lord Jesus comes with love.

The Rosary is for this: that it would be lived with, from youth to death. It is not permitted to omit any of the mysteries, but it is necessary to link each one with the tenth. In us, there must follow a Christ-like surrendering of self to crucifixion, with complete certitude, that in this is love. Only from the crucifixion of his own "I" from the death of the old man, can one begin what is said in the words: "With Christ I am nailed to the Cross".

Let you rejoice and be glad. The Lord Jesus in the greatest suffering preceding the Crucifixion, and in that same Crucifixion, had the joy of knowing that the Redemption was being accomplished. The Mother of God, in the moment of parting with the Lord Jesus and in the time of torment when with the greatest pain she stood under the Cross, had the joy of knowing that this was being accomplished and was accomplished.

When one disposes oneself for the cross and suffering it is possible to acquire this state where one will conform to the Lord Jesus through apostolic ardour. Giving one's hands for nailing it is possible to save souls, but it is necessary to know that by lifting pins from the ground it is also possible to save souls. (St. Therese). This is neither a phrase nor an exaggeration.

90. I am humbling myself before the Most Holy Mother of the Word Incarnate and the King.

I am asking for a gracious glance of your Maternal

Eyes, of which I am not worthy, but I have the right as a sinner – for such love the Holy Trinity created you, formed you, and gave you.

I am asking, and at the same time I am giving thanks, for this gift of forgiveness of sins through your Son, for which I am elevating my hands in a single act of trust. I know that my greatest happiness is your greatest joy, and I beseech that through the power of your Heart over the Heart of Jesus, you would obtain from Him this miracle of mercy, and that this act, which I am experiencing, would extend itself for all the living, now and until the end of the world, and would endure forever in Heaven, in order that, in it, God, Who is Love, would be adored by everybody.

And now there will be this which decides the essence of the condition of the first Saturdays – Rosary meditation.

There is no child who comes to his Mother with a flower, with a gift, or with something, which is a sign of his love, who would not receive a caress on the head, together with a glance full of goodness, which gives peace and security. With one hand you are giving a recited Rosary – with the other you are taking graces to the heart. You are speaking about love – keep in mind these words: *"You are all beautiful and worthy of all praise". "I am the Mother of Beautiful love, and of awe, and of piety and of holy hope",* and as it is in the hymn: *"All the gifts which are in Heaven God poured out on you, Virgin, as a rich garment from the sun, and from the stars a crown woven for your head......"*

Each of the fifteen mysteries is a mystery of love. It is necessary to consider this often by the means already

The SECRET POWER of the ROSARY

known to you: we are uniting in the mutual love of Both Most Holy Hearts in Their love of God the Father, of the Angels and of all mankind... This is like the turning on of the contact (like electricity) for the adoration, the presentation, and the request for this love.

And now, in the accomplishment of the Redemption, the two last mysteries are coming. The Mother of God became overflowing with the fullness of the effects of the Redemption, such as no other creature. The Mother Most Holy, as the Immaculate Conception – differently, but more perfectly, with the greatest merit, with love and the surrendering of self to the Will of God – utilised the Redemption, and on this way, she calls everyone. The Mother of God desires only this: the glory of God and the salvation of souls. It is *Omnipotentia orans* (Almighty praying) and therefore, it has to have that which is necessary, which helps, which asks, and which she gave to humanity – this is *Oratio Omnipotens* (the Almighty Prayer) this is **THE ROSARY**. *"And I took root in an honest nation….."* In the Rosary there is Mary, *Rosa Mystica* (Mystical Rose) and *Eerva Dei* (Handmaid of God) who offers *Rosarium* (The Rosary) as *Servitam Dei* (Servant of God) from those from whom she herself took root. This is the mystery of the desire for the Rosary and of the importance of the Rosary. This is the mystery of the promise that through the well-said Rosary one redeems. This is in Holy Scripture: *"He who finds Me – finds life and draws salvation from the Lord".* Mary is in the Rosary, and through the Rosary we find her. This is the drawing out of salvation. The Rosary is through Mary *for us*, and through Mary *for Heaven.*

91. Do not fear; drink from the spring, which never dries up, which this devotion is. From the spring of life are the waters of the graces of the Rosary, because my Son chose this way for their dispensation. Therefore, such opposition, resistance, covering up with something else, disrespect, misunderstanding, and many other reasons, that even those who, in their own opinion, are conquering this devotion, are not quenching the demand, because they are drawing as if with a perforated sieve, although they still know and feel that there is something there. Through humility and the desire to cherish each one, one can clean oneself, refresh, delight and quench the thirst of the sticking lips, and wash oneself with the fullness of both outstretched hands.

Let it not surprise anyone when amazement will seize those who do not have a sense of the mysteries of the Rosary. When one says: "We are offering a decade for this or that", this is not only one Lord's Prayer and ten Angelic Greetings, but there must also be the giving of the possibility of action to the Angels of this given mystery, through its verbal significance and its experience in the soul, even though it would be the least fragment of thought, of heart, or even an incompetent idea, or even though it would be only a statement in the will. But there must be, somehow, a unity even though it would be but a single thread, between the interior of a person and the given mystery and its Angel. Let it not surprise those who know. Let them, humbly, give thanks, and thus faithfully, Oh how faithfully, they cooperate with the given graces. And seized with amazement will be those who in the Scripture are astonished: *"These are those whom, in contempt, we regarded as fools".*

Now, let you take into yourselves this fifteenth mystery. In it you have the Queen and Mother. How pleased a child on earth would be, if his Mother – who had lived a silent and despised life, with sacrifice and overflowing suffering – received reward and royal dignity! May the memory of this mystery be your joy, and may happiness, rapture and thanksgiving overflow your breasts. Thanks be to the Lord God Most High for the grace, which is the greatest grace, which the Creator gave to His Own creature, and which is the sign of His greatest justice. Oh, do not fear her – you, who desire only perfect faithfulness in the slavery of Love. *„Idzie, idzie Bóg prawdziwy, idzie sędzia sprawiedliwy". ("The true God comes, the just judge comes").* With the highest justice is the highest dimension of reward. And the reward is an act of justice for the acceptance of grace – the Will of God.

92. The taking away of fear is a grace, but the acceptance of it is the acceptance of the Cross, the acceptance of suffering. But in order that it would be meritorious it must be in peace, and with a loving fiat.

It is not necessary for anything to act violently in the soul. It is necessary in the sorrowful part of the Rosary, and at its stations, to ponder and to penetrate this, which from people, is most hidden: the joy of Both Most Holy Hearts from the fulfilment of the Redemption. This joy, most deeply hidden, but yet most essential, is really out of love for God, Whose Majesty was implored, and out of love for souls. This is truth. Therefore, he who is from God seeks truth and comprehends it, and his heart expands with happiness.

The Lord Jesus, bidding farewell to His friends, knew that for which He Himself was going and for which they were waiting. Alone, He took on Himself the suffering of fear in the Garden, and to them He said: ***"Let not your hearts be troubled; do not fear."*** This latent joy in the torment of the Saviour and in the united suffering of His Mother Most Holy, is a sign of the true brothers and sisters and children of Jesus and Mary. Is this not also necessary, for every moment, for the slaves of love?

There has to be hatred of evil and of sin. When one penetrates well into the pain in the five mysteries of the Rosary then sin is annihilated. It is like this: when one writes out another word on an inscribed word, the previous word is not present, and it is not even possible to make it out. How easy it is, therefore, to stamp on the words: pardon, mercy, grace, and peace – so that the previous letters of the words will no longer be possible to find again. But when this will happen in time, is not your concern. Faith suffices that in this moment it is happening. However, it is possible to happen visibly before death, or only to be glanced at by the Holy Angels before judgement, in the last moment for which they are waiting in trembling expectation for a new fire to explode, which would be thankful, and would adore their Angelic Source.

Everyone does not comprehend this immediately, but souls, simple and humble, find in this meditation much consolation. Amen.

93.   The reign establishes the end of the road in eternity, and it already endures eternally. Each one who fulfils the

The SECRET POWER of the ROSARY

Will of God, which is destined for him, takes such a road to this place, and to this degree of glory, which has to endure eternally. And the way has to be very similar, and even as much as possible similar to Mary's way, because it is united with the way of the Most Holy Virgin, and in each mystery of the Rosary it is necessary to seek Mary, and in Mary to seek oneself. It is necessary to know and to think about this, that striving to accomplish salvation and holiness gives the greatest glory to God, and therefore, this is our obligation in relation to the Lord God. The less thought about self and activity for self, the greater will be the giving of glory to God the most High. This same thing may have the appearances of good done badly, or indifferently (which already is badly), or perfectly.

In this last mystery lies the secret, that the self-annihilation of the Mother Most Holy in the first mystery of the Rosary was the reason and the necessity for the end, which is the glory and the reign that is now her privilege. This self-annihilation of the Mother Most Holy has its own expression in the seeming omission of her from some mysteries of her Rosary, and it is necessary only to look for her in each of them, and to compare oneself to her.

Today's meditations establish an indication of how to utilise the Rosary daily. This is the mystery of holiness, because it contains in itself the teaching about the half-dead seed and about the cross of annihilation by St. John of the Cross. Direct everything to God for His Glory, and seek God in the neighbour, and this has to be done in Mary, with Mary, through Mary, and for Mary, and then the crowning takes place. Every least disordered thought about self is like a spit on a dish. Each act of ours, done with grace, serving

133

for eternity, is dispatched, not only for the storing, but also for adaptation for a crown for us. At the court of the Queen everyone has to have a crown, a distinction, and striving for the most beautiful – gives glory to the Queen. But these crowns are, as it were with secret signs, the written history of the struggle with the enemy who lies in wait for these jewels, and they are also the safe conduct for entry to the Kingdom of Glory. Such a crown is already destined for us there, but it is not possible for it to be made if the gold, the stones, and the pearls are not supplied. To end, a further caution: that through the stealing in, or the admittance, of regard for oneself alone in any act or affair whatever, one can easily exchange gold for metal, a diamond for a pebble, and pearls for chaff. The Joy of the Kingdom of Mary is the preparation of the most beautiful crowns for her children.

94.   For acceptance of the Cross, the Lord Jesus prepared with prayer in the Garden. This preparation of the Lord Jesus for the Passion – this perfect prayer – is a source of grace for us. Peace and power. Fear and fright were also sufferings, which the Lord Jesus took upon Himself. First of all the Lord Jesus gave His own consent for the Cross, later there was the taking of the Cross, the carrying of the Cross, the falls beneath the Cross and so on, to the end.

We often have to exercise self-control, and whether through acts of the will, surrender, or the surmounting of self we are agreeing to accept each cross. It is necessary to include this command with meditation on all of the Sorrowful Mysteries. How, most of all, should we think about the Lord Jesus? For this there is no other way possible than only to continually drive into one's head the Sorrowful Mysteries.

The peace, which some people accept as an attitude in the face of persecution, in the face of harm and suffering, in the face of the possibility of something worse, is not possible to explain otherwise than only through their desire to attribute to themselves this merit: that they are without fear, that they are not afraid. And anyone who lives with the mysteries of the Holy Rosary can even fear without sin, if his own fear is united with the fear of the Lord Jesus in the first sorrowful mystery. This means that our temptation has to unite with those, which the Lord Jesus conquered and rejected. When we unite our own fears with the fears of the Lord Jesus – then it will not be of profit to satan to torment us with this temptation, and so it departs.

To unite joy with the joy of the Mother of God, it is necessary only to continually combine it to oneself thus: When guests are coming, or when we are going to people, it is necessary to be with the Mother of God of the first joyful mystery of the domestic life of the family, and to connect this with the fifth. The joy of a soul after Confession is also union with the fifth. Enchantment and astonishment, many times the secret activity of God, reveals itself to us in great or little individual events – with the first because this is, as it were, a continuation of the Divine plan in which the Mother of God was brought into this mystery, and we somehow are making a continuation of this. The happiness from the reception of Holy Communion, from giving to another, and from sharing graces with others, are to be united with the first and third mysteries.

The joy from apostolic success we are to unite with

the birth of the Lord Jesus through Mary, and with the joy, which Mary experienced with the arrival of the Shepherds and the Three Kings.

- Fears – with the fears of the Lord Jesus.
- Fear, weakness suffering, physical pain – with the seventh mystery.
- Insult and calumny – with the eighth.
- All wrongs, injustices – with the sorrowful mysteries.

And so on, one can thus apply crosses, and one's own way of the Cross to the Way of the Cross of the Lord Jesus. The pain of separation when we lose someone close, when one looks at the death of another, or when one dies to oneself – is to be united with the tenth, but immediately one should hasten to the twelfth. When through Mary we receive new flows of the fires and lights of the Holy Spirit, when our hearts extend with happiness consisting in knowledge – this is tied in with the thirteenth. Joy, which even for a moment we ought not to abandon, joy from belonging to the Holy Church, joy from the grace of Baptism, from all the sacraments – with the fifteenth. It is possible to consider one thing from many sides. By this means, when with humility and not trusting in himself somebody tries to live with the Rosary every second of life and death, then Mary becomes indispensable to him, and likewise to the last breath of his life. And in this way, the Rosary goes as far as contemplation.

As one has Mary in the memory, and has the skill of adaptation of the mysteries to life, and of life to the mysteries, then this is the end of the silly smiles, and no ugly word, through thoughtlessness, goes out from the lips, and neither is it possible to make a person lose his patience. It is necessary that people would know that they should say the Rosary most simply, and thus they will experience it most simply, and then it becomes that which is the condition for entry into the Kingdom of God.

95. From my *Fiat* in the first joyful mystery, through *Fiat voluntas tua* in the first sorrowful to *"It is accomplished"* in the tenth mystery – behold how a person in his own life, from joy, through torment to death, has to unite himself with Us, and from the degree of his love depends the degree of his unity with Us. For everything a time comes. People do not think, or think little, about this. But well-said Rosaries teach them about this, and lead and help them, so that in the greatest pain, and in the greatest sacrifice, through everything, and above everything, the Glorious Mysteries – which establish the final goal – would triumph!

Let you remember my words, that before I put their souls as flowers before the Divine Throne, first I will come at death with all the graces for salvation. (Fatima revelation). These are those, who accepted my promise with thanksgiving, fulfilling it obediently and with love, and who are looking forward to its fulfilment with joy. As long as you have time – let you try to propagate this teaching with the living and written word, with acts of example, and above all with prayer and sacrifice, in order that the desire of my Heart, of bestowing this privilege in the greatest possible quantity to souls, would be appeased.

96. You desired. Therefore I am here. I come to bring this, which I desire, and to give this, which I have promised. The Rosary is mine. In it is contained the range of my life on earth, and a piece is put aside in Heaven, where each act of love on earth is crowned. My beautiful crown is adorned with a multitude of pearls and stones – these are the virtues and merits, in which you all have to have a share.

A child, at the sight of a treasure inaccessible to himself, falls into rapture, and directly, there arises in him a desire to own it. The same goes for you. In the Rosary it is possible to recognise gifts, such as the love of the Most Holy Trinity which was poured on me – because it so pleased the Lord. And directly when the desire arises – as with the child – to draw it out with the hand, then already it is possible to enrich oneself: *"Come and eat your fill of My fruits"*, and in humility and happiness, thanking the Lord God for it, with me and for me, you become the owners of these gifts, and although they surpass the immensity and value of all the world, there is room enough for them in each human heart. And the greatest gift of my Heart, which shines in each of the fifteen mysteries – is my unity with the Most Sacred Heart of my Son and King, in which your hearts have to have a share. Through saying: *"Hail Mary, full of grace, the Lord is with thee"* you have a share in bringing to me the greeting, through the Archangel, from the throne of the Divine Majesty.

Let you return, often, to this most simple meditation in rapture and humility: *"Hail Mary, full of grace"*. Let you live with this. My Son, Whom I carry in my Heart, listens with joy to these words, because always, He desires that which He announced to the world in the words: "Jesus desires, that I would be more known and loved." (Fatima). The Pope confirmed this revelation; the words are those of the Lord Jesus; he who hears them has to fulfil them – as the Most Holy Will – with all of his heart, with all of his strength, and with the whole soul. Woe, if it not. In the light of these words, which are what the Lord desires of the world, this has to be a criterion for you in many matters, to judge their kind, their origin, and their goal

97.   The Rosary begins in the first mystery with an act of love, of obedience, an act of consent and the act of faith of the Mother of God, and in the fifteenth it ends with her triumph, coronation and reign. If one looks at the first mystery, it is ***"Non hirruisti Virginus uterum" (You did not spurn the Lord's dwelling place in life).*** And in the fifteenth this is the King of kings and the Lord of lords, and the Son, giving the reward of glory. We have to serve with Mary in this way, in order that the reception of the reward of glory would be possible for us from the same Lord Jesus, only. (Not from the world).

It is necessary, according to the command, to prepare the soul for the prayer of the Rosary through great self-annihilation before the Lord, but also through a strong, trusting and constant enduring act of faith in the power and efficacy of the Rosary, and after its ending it is necessary to make an act of thanksgiving for the holy Angels having carried it, and for this they will, for certain, carry it.

And furthermore – it is necessary to remind oneself and to exhort others: Let you love the Rosary! Revere it! Trust in its power of the merits of the entire Redemption! Let you protect its mysteries. Let you defend it from all evil. Rejoice in it, as the precious treasure, which with rapturous heart, can each day unfold with the fingers. Let you kiss it. Have it on your person! Share it with others, because one does not become poor through this, but becomes rich.

98. The Rosary is the criterion of holiness. When someone who says the Rosary is not holy, this is not the fault of the Rosary, but of how it is said. When the Queen of the Rosary promises something she keeps her word. The Holy Rosary gives holy wisdom, power, and perseverance to those who cherish the Lord's Coming.

The Rosary has to prepare the Lord's Coming. The Rosary gives a holy desire for holiness, the sign of which is a desire for the Kingdom of God here on earth, for the reign of Jesus and Mary, and the desire for the Kingdom of God in Heaven, and the desire to be there already.

The way to this is true judgement about all matters here on earth. The Rosary gives truth to judgement about all matters here on earth. On its basis is cast out what is satanical, and it raises up beyond the earth, and our intercourse truly reaches to the Heavens.

99. I am here – we are together.

The mystery of the Resurrection follows immediately after the sorrowful mysteries. It is not necessary to delay on sufferings, but to run out with all one's soul, this is, with thought and heart, to the desire for the triumph over death, hell and satan. Christ accomplished the Resurrection through His Divine Power. Trust and surrender yourself to the action of this Divine Power, through my hands.

After the Assumption my Immaculate Heart burned with unspeakable joy from the fact that the Lord God had already appointed a time for me. The Most Holy Trinity desired this joy for my Heart – for each of you, and for everyone. And this is precisely what is necessary for each one to have in the heart when leaving the world. It is necessary to desire the glory of God to the same extent that one desires the happiness of one's own salvation.

The Glorious part of the Rosary has to become, for each one, a preparation for eternal happiness. And when it is difficult to meditate, it is necessary to awaken this intention generally before saying this part, or before individual decades. This has to prepare and to purify – through the Immaculate Heart, through imitation of It, through graces asked from It and through love – the term of the earthly pilgrimage, the happy term of the earthly pilgrimage. All of this through the Immaculate Heart, to which one should often call: *Janua Caelli – ora pro nobis. (Gate of Heaven – pray for us).* Amen

100. The world is deprived of love of God the Father. God the Father is shoved away by people. It is necessary to repair this.

The Rosary has to be with everything. The Rosary

has to be everything. *Noverim me – noverim Te. (May I know myself – may I know You).* **"Because God so loved the world that He gave His Only Begotten Son so that everyone who believes in Him will not die but will have eternal life."** (John 3.16). *And therefore, it is necessary to examine* all the mysteries of the Redemption in the light of the love of God the Father for the Son, and for the most perfect of all His creatures – Mary, and also for the Angels, for St. Joseph and for all the people saying the Rosary by this means. This draws us very near to the world of the supernatural.

People stimulate thoughts about the love of the Lord Jesus, and of the Most Holy Mother and the Angels, for God the Father – and we have to love God the Father through the inclusion of our love in the love of both Most Sacred Hearts. I love You, Father, with the Heart of Your Son, surrendered to You and loving You in the mystery of the Annunciation … The Nativity … The Crucifixion … and so on. In the individual Sorrowful Mysteries it is necessary to consider the love of the Father for the Son, suffering, and for His sorrowful Mother. God the Father loves His suffering Son; His Son dying on the Cross, and His Mother; and He loves you in your suffering. Can it be otherwise? Do you believe this? This ought to prepare people, so that they would not have resentment, when punishments come. Speak to them about this, briefly, simply and strongly.

God the Father looks with great love on the Son in the Womb of Mary, and the Son gives glory and love to the Father. The Father loves us when the Lord Jesus lives in us. God the Father loves St. Joseph, Zechariah, Elizabeth – all

The SECRET POWER of the ROSARY

are in the scope of His Great Love. This is one method.

The second method: In each mystery – The Lord Jesus is this, the Mother of God is this – and I? What am I? *Noverim me*. This is the constant daily reckoning of the conscience in the Rosary. This helps towards knowledge of self in the Divine Light, because everything, and each situation, is in the mysteries of the Rosary.

St. Louis Grignon de Montfort indicates the virtue in a given mystery and asks for it. This is the third means – the desire of virtue. This is very easy; this each one, himself, fills up with his own essence, and this is important, because this is the way to contemplation, although it comes about, as it were, unintentionally, as if one went for a walk and reached the summit, but not like this: with a rucksack, climbing irons, lines, and later a wind drifted – and nothing came of it.

Emotions in the Rosary:

1. It is not possible to put up dams.
2. We must ask for them.
3. In meditation emotion is kindled. We must try for emotion and accept it as a Divine gift.
4. Being in dryness I say "I love You, God", and then, with the will, I strive for emotion.
5. Through the Rosary, love will be enkindled, because in the Rosary there is meditation.

Through reading the Gospels, as well as with such saying of the Rosary, we will have the life of the Lord Jesus and the Mother of God in ourselves, and we will be giving it to others, and the world will change quickly and easily. With the saying of the Rosary the Holy Spirit is drawn down and "renews the face of the earth."

101. I have to pay homage to the Blessed Virgin Mary, in the first mystery of the Incarnation, as the Queen of Angels who, from the Archangel Gabriel, receives the greeting of the Most Holy Trinity which made the announcement of all the graces which are flowing on the Mother of God, and which confirmed, as it were, the authorization to the graces which the Mother of God had already experienced, but she was unaware of their cause. In this mystery there is the joy and adoration of all the Heavenly Spirits from the happiness of owning such a Queen.

In the Visitation the action of the Holy Angels: their activity with the spirit of prophecy with St. Elizabeth: *"Blessed are thou ... "*and also about the action of the Holy Angels in the untying of the penalty of the powerless tongue of Zechariah. And again the happiness, glory and love of all the Angels, which they offered to God in thanksgiving for the giving to them of Mary for Queen and Virgin, as well as for her action.

The third mystery – new happiness – which it is not possible to express. The Angels experienced happiness from her Motherhood of God and its effects for them to the end of the ages on earth, and for eternity in Heaven.

In the Presentation and the Finding, in the hidden life of the Divine Saviour, and of the entire Holy Family – so immeasurable, unspeakable, inconceivable for our minds and hearts – the joy of the Angels taking part in their life.

The SECRET POWER of the ROSARY

They knew, that this is their Queen; they had this announced, not as announced to people, they had this shown!

And so it is necessary to meditate in all the fifteen mysteries on how the Holy Angels who took part in them acted, knowing the privileges, graces and the action of their Queen.

The fulfilment of the happiness of the Angels, the fullness of their happiness – behold what is accomplished in the mysteries of the Assumption and the Coronation.

Just as the Redemption of humankind was fulfilled in all of these mysteries, likewise for the Angels, the fulfilment of this happiness – to which they attained the right through the victory – followed in all of these fifteen mysteries.

They knew their Queen and Virgin, as well as her work, and this intensified their happiness. And in them this endures.

And we, particularly in August but also later, with the saying of the Rosary, have to know, to adore, our Virgin and Queen and her work in the Redemption. This has to become our happiness here, and it will endure, also, forever. Through such meditation, vigilance, and adoration of the Immaculate Heart of Mary, of Its activity in each of the mysteries, we will fulfil the desire of the Lord Jesus, that His Most Holy Mother would be more known and loved. This, one should fulfil through saying the Rosary well.

In each "Hail" one worships, and in each retained thought one knows, and in each mystery one receives graces to the heart, and the goal of all these graces is love, which endures forever.

God is Love. The Lord Jesus came to start a fire on earth, and He wished that it would be enflamed. And the fire of love already here on earth unites with the love in Heaven and this establishes the beginning of eternal life, because, when the time comes when faith and hope are established this love is, and endures forever.

I am adding in conclusion: For help in love, knowledge, service, self-giving, activity, sacrifice, suffering, adoration and thanksgiving we have in the Rosary, and for all our earthly life, the Holy Angels from the nine choirs, given to us by their Queen. May God be adored in His Angels and in His Saints.

102. Through the pious saying of the Rosary we assure for ourselves the help of the Mother of God at the hour of death. In the Rosary one says: *"Holy Mary, Mother of God, pray for us sinners now and at the hour of our death."* This is repeated 150 times – *now* and at the hour of *death.* Now, already it is necessary to think about the last things, with the Rosary in the hand, praying for the state of grace, for perseverance, and for a happy death.

This which is terrifying for people – the wall with the unknown writing – when we consider it with the Rosary in hand it becomes pleasant and attractive, so that the most earthly-minded people begin to reach out their hands towards their own end.

The fourteenth mystery – The Mother of God taken up to Heaven. Those who love each other wish to be together; a loving child wishes to be with its Mother. Because one knows that the Mother Most Holy is in Heaven, this longing and desire can arise in the heart as a response to the thought about death. The glory of Mary is the greatest adornment of Heaven.

These thoughts have for their purpose the mitigation of such brief sounding, yet terrible in their irreversibility, words: death, judgement, Heaven or hell.

103. *"O Mary conceived without sin"*. This is an abbreviation of the entire Rosary to a few words. *"Hail Mary, full of grace"* – the source of this fullness of grace is the conception without sin. And what is in the Rosary? *"Pray for us sinners now and at the hour of our death"*. – But this also means: *"Pray for us who have recourse to thee."*

"Blessed is the fruit of thy womb, Jesus." Although you may be tired, distracted, occupied with the greatness of the affairs of this world, with the pronouncing of my name, *"Mary"* and later with the words *"the fruit of thy womb, Jesus"* – at which every knee kneels – let you remember as you pronounce these two names of the Mother and Son, to put into it love and honour, awe and childlike sweetness, trust and longing – and, even if only with these two Names, to desire to unite in thought and in heart with me and My Son. How different these, your Rosaries, would be, and how easy it would be by this means; so simple and accessible even for the smallest child who pronounces them! How easy it would be to enlarge and deepen your vessels for the hoarding of the graces contained in the Rosary!

Who, saying this greeting, which is called Angelic, thinks about death? But after all the second part is precisely a petition with a recollection of death; about the hour of death.

When saying the Rosary as a whole let you think – even many times about each mystery – that each of them is an indispensable part of your Redemption, and they are the means which demonstrates the accomplishment of this Redemption. And the great thanksgiving – this emotion so pleasing to the Lord, which through all my earthly life and now in Heaven, fills my Heart – will fill yours also.

In the Resurrection one should think about the power, about this singular miracle, about this almighty power shattering hell and death. Hence trust, peace, and joy penetrating all creation, which came from God, and which praises God. Hence, there is only one proper attitude to the enemies (speech here about devils) – contempt.

104. The ninth mystery – the pre-death way of the Lord Jesus.

"If you do not do penance – you shall all perish."

These are the words of the Lord Jesus. The Lord Jesus goes on this terrible way; the Mother of God with Him – beside Him.

All those who regard their own way of life as a crossing over, have the Mother of God with them as the easiest base for crossing to eternity. The Mother of God desires that we would remember about the Way of the Lord Jesus and her way, because one elevation of thought towards this mystery opens the floodgates of graces. The Mother of God with her Son, beside Him and most closely united with Him, obtains for us, by entreaty, unceasing graces, even those for which we do not pray.

We find everything for this mystery in the Gospels. The Mother of God wishes that we would be living with this. Then our Way of the Cross will be just as it has to be, as it ought to be: because if you will not do penance, you will all perish. *"If someone wishes to follow Me, let him deny himself; let him take his cross and follow after Me."* And therefore it is good to live through this ninth mystery with the words of the Gospel. This means that we would look at the Lord Jesus Who falls, goes, falls, and Who is fed with hatred and sneering, and Who is disdained. These are apparently the simplest things, which each one knows, but one ought to live with it. *"Jesus, meek and humble of heart, make our hearts like unto Your Heart."*

When the Way of the Cross comes for a person, generally he has not got a friend, only the Mother of God. The Mother of God is with us then on the entire Way of the Cross of our lives, if only we have these same intentions as the Lord Jesus. Penance is the fulfilment of the Will of God. The teaching about the dry and green wood also refers to this mystery.

"My yoke is sweet, and My burden is light." This happens when one chooses the way to Heaven from the Lord God, through the Mother of God. This is about the Cross and our relation to it, me, and her relation to us – to each one of us. And this signifies the world – hatred, scoffing, curiosity, expectation, ingratitude, and lack of sympathy. *"As they hated Me they will also hate you."* The Mother of God is on the Way of the Cross and meets, comes out to meet, Her Son burdened with the Cross. If we also wish to walk in the footsteps of the Lord Jesus and we

accept the Will of the Father with reverence and peace, then we always meet the Mother of God on our Way of the Cross. Mother Most Holy, Most Sorrowful! We love you with all our heart!

105. *"Wine which Virgin bears..."*
"Bread of the strong..."

I am the Virgin Queen. Virginity is my great privilege for the preservation and celebration of which God performed the miracle of my Divine Motherhood. In the month of May in many different quarters of the globe people are singing litanies and calling to me: *"Queen of Virgins, pray for us!"*

The world disdains virginity, and the devils are doing everything in order to lead to the earliest possible destruction of it, both of soul and body, in the embryo. Therefore, I demanded the souls of virgins in Fatima who would consciously accept and carry this cross, which is hidden in lilies for love of me. But now, also, priests stupefied, and absorbed in worldliness and sensuality, advise that this cross would be thrown out, and they do not wish to make this sacrifice, which is the great honor and privilege, to pay for the sacrament of the priesthood. And when this has a place, even though it would be only in their minds and wills – already the inheritance has become destroyed.

All this results from a lack of acquaintance with me, from a lack of love towards me, from a lack of seeking me, from a lack of entreaty for love; and all this is on account of relinquishment of the Rosary; because this is like a knot which when released causes everything to be opened wide.

and it is easy for the enemy to conquer.

Let you believe in the Rosary, give the Rosary, proclaim and propagate the message which you have received from me about the Rosary. Let you love the Rosary, live with it, and above all let you say it in humility, with strong faith, with limitless trust, burning with pure *love*, and with the perseverance which wins Heaven. Amen.

106.　*"Take off your shoes, because the place where you are standing is holy."* These words refer to Gietrzwałd, Warminsko, where in the year 1877 the Mother of God revealed herself as the Immaculate Conception.

"O Mary conceived without sin, pray for us who have recourse to thee." Because I am without sin I pray for you sinners. My privilege, my right and my happiness is the bringing of sinners to my Son, most merciful. But I bring them, as it were, with a loop from a chain laid on the neck, in order to draw them with this. This loop is the Rosary. And in the Rosary is totality – the totality of the Redemption. With each Rosary that is said we protect and enclose this place with a circle. Perhaps nowhere else, as here, has the Mother of God related her desire for the saying of the Rosary with a place: that here, the Rosary should reverberate continually.

Because the Mother of God manifested herself here as the Immaculate, therefore, in this place we think about the Assumption. These two dogmas are strongly tied together, but they have to become still more tied into one totality through the expected dogma of Mediatrix of all graces.

The Immaculate Conception, The Assumption, The Coronation, Mediatrix of all graces: "Come to me everyone, and eat your fill of my fruits" – of the fruits which penetrate from the privilege of the Immaculate Conception.

Whoever will desire the fruits of the Mother Most Holy, will at the same time have the desire: of greater purity, of greater humility, of greater love of Christ the Saviour, of Truth, of greater love of Christ in the neighbour, of a great desire for the glory of God and the salvation of souls, of great and entire surrendering of self to God with confidence in His wisdom and love and in the power of His Divine Omnipotence, as well as of a great tearing away of self from the worthless matters of this life.

Whoever, saying the Rosary, has a heart filled with requests, these are, through the utterance of the Angelic Greetings, spontaneously intertwined in this Rosary. That is why, when the Angels are delivering a recited Rosary to the Blessed Mother, all these requests are intertwined in this wreath. It is not necessary to say that this Hail Mary is for this, for this, or for that.

The presentation of requests to the Mother Most Holy is at the same time a giving of glory to Her, and the Lord Jesus likes this. Little Rosary people are poor, but everything is so arranged, that they are giving glory to the Blessed Mother.

From these very brief meditations there has to penetrate a still greater love of the Immaculate Conception, of the Assumption of the Mother of God and of Her Rosary, a greater understanding of the action of the Rosary and of the privileges of the Immaculate Conception, a greater desire for the utilisation of time for prayer and the Rosary apostolate, which the Mother of God here particularly blesses.

107.   The Rosary is the Mother of God's gift, and the Rosary is the Mother of God's requirement. As one accepts it, so one already gives it. How miserable is this, which we are giving in the face of that which we receive. Why do people wish, by satan's means, to make it complex?

If there is any prayer in which all the most glaring deficiencies and praying errors arise, it is precisely in the Rosary. I will tell you metaphorically: Now I see race-horses. These are evil spirits in haste with the Rosary. I see animals in grass, neither ass nor calf, completely black. Calf, ass; stupid animals; it is said: "Stupid as an ass" or "stupid as a calf." This refers to those who thoughtlessly chatter the Rosary.

Because this is September we say the Sorrowful Mysteries. It is necessary to consider about this, that the Mother of God is a sea of sorrow. Yes! In this saying there is not an overstatement, rather a deficit – let us take for example the separation before the accomplishment of the Redemption.

Each movement of the Heart of the Mother of God is an inconceivable ocean of merits, which are the treasure of the Church, and therefore, the endurance of sufferings by us, in union with Mary, and for Mary, becomes also for us the opening of great merits; only through lack of silence and humility of heart we lose them. The Mother of God has immense sympathy for each suffering heart, and through her own sufferings she became Comforter of the Afflicted, the Mother of Consolation, and this flows out from the Rosary.

Would that the fifteen mysteries and all the invocations of the Litany of Loreto were undertaken. This latter contains in itself all the titles and privileges of the Mother of God which are in the Rosary, only they are not mentioned, and therefore, the Litany of Loreto is very important and very pleasing to the Lord Jesus. This has a connection with the manifestation in Heede.

The sorrowful Heart of the Mother Most Holy in each of the sorrowful mysteries, and even in the fourth and fifth joyful mysteries, shows us her most wonderful holiness in the most perfect acceptance and submission, in the most perfect endurance and unity, in the most perfect silence and humility of heart in the most perfect of all creatures.

We, who so succeed to sympathise with creatures in different situations of life, have such hardness of heart when it comes to making recompense to God. How good it is, that the Mother of God, in the prophecy of Simeon, in the flight to Egypt, in the seeking and finding of the Son, and in all the Sorrowful Mysteries is so near to us, so human, and at the same time, so majestic and so great. She confers on us that which is necessary in suffering, which she knows... which she experiences... the Mother of God laments. We must, therefore, find in each suffering heart some part of the sufferings of her Heart in our neighbour.

And lastly, what I wish to say is that we have to value pain, to regard it as a great gift, as a privilege of a particular kind. Inasmuch as we will have such an attitude in the face of pain it will already be different; it will remove this blade, which satan would wish to remain. It becomes transformed from the level of evil – of satan – and at once it goes into something Divine. In pain, there is the greatest humility, and therefore satan does not comprehend this, and never will understand it, and therefore, is here defeated.

Such is the school of life –
the school of death –
and the school of triumph!

108.   The Rosary is the guide to holiness.

As one says *"Hail Mary"...* one welcomes, greets, and accepts many graces. For that same word, *Mary,* the Church granted a feast. At that same word, *Mary,* satan trembles. At that same word, *Mary,* the Angels rejoice.

As one says *"Full of grace"* this also has a deep meaning, because through the fullness of grace Mary is so closely united with God that when praying to her we are praying to God – together with her.

"The Lord is with thee"

In all of the fifteen mysteries from the Annunciation to the Coronation, we have to consider *"The Lord is with thee".* In each mystery we desire that the Lord would be with us through grace. There, where the Lord finds more of the spirit of Mary, there, He will willingly live with us. Make efforts so that there would not be any moment without grace. All of our drawing near to the Mother of God has for its purpose the realisation of this saying: *"The Lord is with thee".*

All of the approaches of the Mother of God to the world, to all the people, are for this – that the Lord God would be able to be with us. All the mysteries of the Rosary – all the fifteen decades – are a reaching out of the hand to God, Who draws near to us and induces us to the cause of the Mother of God, so that we are not cleaned off from the surface of the earth – this is also her cause. All our service to the Mother Most Holy is so that the gain for ourselves would be – that the Lord God would be with us. But the Mother of God desires that we would serve her as she wishes, and not as we would wish, and therefore, meditation on the mysteries of the Rosary very much helps in the imitation of her, and through this, to the easiest means of salvation.

We have St. Therese, and her *"Little Way"* which she showed to the world, is the way of the Mother of God: the most perfect fulfilment of the smallest things, with love.

The entire way of the Mother of God was precisely such. All the things that the Mother of God did so simply, were ordinary, but only in the eyes of the world. The Mother of God had an Infant, and earthly mothers have infants, but the difference is like that between Heaven and earth. We ought to do ordinary things, following the example of Jesus and Mary in the mysteries of the Rosary, that is, to unite with the intention which is extraordinary in these mysteries, which is – Divine. The devil does not wish this; he hates this. And each one can find this for himself in each of the mysteries, depending on the needs of his own life. Saints of different epochs, such as St. Therese of the Child Jesus, St. Louis de Montfort, and the Seraphic St. Francis, accomplished and demonstrated to us that it is possible to be thus united with God. They, with their own happiness already here on earth, are drawing people to this unity.

The complete thought about this is as follows: Mary endures poverty, difficulties, the work of family life, of ordinary life, seeking the Child, and so on. It is necessary to do ordinary things, we must do them, and this is indispensable, as clearly seen in the usual aspects of the life of Jesus and Mary in the mysteries of the Rosary. But because we know that their life is Divine, therefore, we have to have the intention of uniting our usualness of life with the unusualness of the mysteries of the Rosary with which one

adores God,

conquers satan,

and saves souls.

He who understands this finds, in the Rosary, the guide to holiness.

109. The second mystery: In it, also, one finds everything which is necessary in order to imitate Mary in regard to God and to people.

Many a time people think that the Mother of God went to St. Elizabeth with the same kind of haste with which people hurry. But with her there was nothing negative in the haste. This refers to the immediateness of the fulfilment of that which God desired of her. In this is contained her attitude to the Will of God. She knows that Elizabeth will have a son, and that this is something extraordinary. She knows that God wishes her to be there – so she goes. When they met they both were filled with happiness – St. Elizabeth and the Mother of God infinitely exalted. They were pleased with each other's graces and they adored God for them. It is necessary to bring this into relief. There, there is the love towards St. Elizabeth, but above all it is love towards God. We have therefore, naturally, to ennoble well our actions.

The feast of the Visitation is about St. John. *"And you, child, will be called the prophet of the Most High"*. In all human births it is necessary that women would understand that they have a great part in the fulfilment of the plans of God. The crimes of mothers – is the denial to the Lord God of His action, of His plans in the world. People consider that this is only an offense against the fifth commandment – but this especially attacks the Divine Power in His government of the world, because each person already in the mother's womb is called to something; has his own appointed sphere.

In the mystery of the Visitation the joy of the Mother Most Holy is the understanding of her joy by St. Elizabeth. Later, when the Shepherds and the Three Kings came – this is a continuation of this kind of happiness. But now, the Mother of God has such great joy each time that some soul, in humility and astonishment, sees the outpouring of the graces of God on himself and on others. The knowledge of His graces and thanksgiving for them is also very pleasing to the Lord God.

The Mother of God had this thanksgiving to the Lord for everything. And it is very important, that we should have feelings of thanksgiving for everything, with humility, because this causes joy to both Most Holy Hearts, and it put us in the proper place. Then there is immense joy in the Divine Spirit; and the showing of this in appearance, in the expression of the face, establishes the evidence that in the heart there is thanksgiving to the Lord God. I am not worthy of this – but the Lord gives this to me – therefore, thanksgiving!

In the Visitation is the sanctification by the Mother Most Holy and the Word Incarnate, of practical matters: joy visited. It is necessary that all our relations with people would be under the power of this mystery; and so few are.

In this mystery we see the punishment of Zechariah directly after sin, and the drawing into light of the greatness of this sin. Included in it is that of which there is so much in our times, namely: the attitude of unbelief towards the supernatural activity of the Lord God. The mute was removed; excluded, through his deformity, from normal life. Later Zechariah spoke, and sang his most beautiful hymn. There are very many like this now, who are in the background, not taking part in the great affairs of God – like a stream flowing nearby them.

Just as the Our Father is the prayer which the Lord Jesus taught us, so the Magnificat is the prayer of the Mother Most Holy, revealing love and thanksgiving, revealing the activity of God: He exalted the humble; He cast down the proud from their thrones; He endowed the poor. This prayer, after the Hail Mary, ought to have such a place, the kind of which is as yet far away from us. It ought to be on the lips and in the heart – the certainty of the promises of the Lord.

We join our Magnificat to the Magnificat of the Mother of God, of St. Elizabeth, of the members of the household, and of all the souls who glorified God with this prayer.

110. The slogan, which through St. Michael the Archangel became the reason for the formation of an entire new family in the Church, (The Congregation of Michaelite Priests), reads:

TEMPERANCE AND WORK.

Work is the conquest of certain impediments and people apply it only to visible things and issues. And meanwhile this, in the first place, has to have application in the sphere of invisible things and affairs.

Work is the conquest of impediments and it must have a goal in order to be work, because if there is not a goal, though it would mean fatigue, it is not work.

The Rosary is work, falling under the senses, and by a certain means being possible to value; and in it there is temperance, because it did not seek a great many and a diversity of words, but confines itself, so to speak, to temper itself to the Lord's Prayer, The Angelic Salutation, and the Glory be to the Father. This is at first glance.

The Rosary is work in the conquest of invisible obstacles, attempting not to give admittance to the utterance of words in which everything is contained. This is the work of thought, of heart, of will, because otherwise, evil would dominate these precise powers. But in this regularity of words, in this constant, day in day out, repeated order of the mysteries in each Rosary, and in the same acceptance of this order, there is, already, merit.

The visible carrying of the Rosary with oneself is the visible sign of this work and temperance.

One ought to ponder and live the slogan "Temperance and Work" through the fifteen mysteries of the Ro-

The SECRET POWER of the ROSARY

sary, and in each of these meditations there comes to light the toil of the work and temperance, such as we have in the most holy plans of the Lord Jesus and His Most Holy Mother. And people should familiarise themselves with this slogan.

The Rosary is the means of reaching the goal about which people have dreamed, about which they have thought, when they spoke about the philosophical stone, which through touch would change everything into gold. My Rosary is the means of changing work into joy and happiness. The Rosary at work, and especially the Rosary said on that same morning, changes work and obligations into the giving of praise and adoration to God and the Most Holy Virgin Mary, and all this is joy.

Just like the true farmer, we have
to sow in joy,
to pray about growth in peace and trust, and
to reap, glorifying the Lord with joy, and
  with a humble heart.

Most important recapitulation:

The work in the saying of the Rosary and all that has been said about temperance – has an unheard-of important meaning with regard to the saying of the Rosary in the morning, and in its entirety, because then it is, as it were, "the Philosophical stone", which changes the entire day, and every matter, into the joy of the fulfilment of penance, which gives the right, with a chaste heart, to adore God, and this is the triumph of God, in the soul and in the world, over evil.

The good accomplishment of this work, and the Rosary well said and offered to God through The Immaculate

Heart of Mary, will change everything into the gold of love. People have believed that such a stone, which when applied changes everything into gold, was nowhere to be found. Behold, in this sphere this is true.

Good prayer is work, and good work is prayer. This transformation of work into prayer, and the action from prayer work – from such good work – is possible only though the Rosary.

The objection that there are too many words in the Rosary, is a swindle. Such an objector, satan has cheated and has achieved his goal. Meanwhile, in the Rosary there is temperance.

In the Rosary also, there is childhood. A child, whether in joy or in suffering, calls his mother, and she only glances at him and knows everything. But an adult interprets and calculates that unless he alone looks after himself he will no longer be able to have anything.

It is necessary to end this meditation by applying to the mysteries of the Rosary the slogan of the Archangel, that a Rosary said thus, effects the opening of a multitude of opportunities till now not perceivable, to temperance itself, and through this to a multitude of sacrifices: of a look, of a word, of a gesture, of an outburst of feeling.

But all this will be formed through meditation on the Rosary, according to the plans and desires of both Most Holy Hearts.

Putting the Rosary in its proper and due place gives the understanding that the cardinal unhappiness is a lack of the Rosary. The reason then of every evil in upbringing is the lack of work on the Rosary. In this lie all the defects in upbringing and the entire incapacity of education.

The SECRET POWER of the ROSARY

111.   The heart is the same as the feelings that are in it, and the feelings are such as the heart hides within it, and it conceals them so that they would not be unpaved by anything from outside, either spiritual or material.

"Set a guard about my mouth and a defensive gate about my lips." And the heart requires, by far, a greater constancy of vigilance for each minute. In the heart of a human, God lives; His Majesty is hiding there – invisible, perceptible. This is true. Therefore, we have to awaken, and to replenish feelings, which have to be directed to God. We have to repeat them until they have become a habit; we have to purify, deepen and ennoble them, and above all, to direct them constantly towards the Lord God and towards His affairs. Such are the Hearts of Jesus and Mary, completely loving, desiring the glory of God and the salvation of souls, as the Will of God.

All other feelings referring to people and their affairs will be properly in their place when they will be directed to the source and the goal, to the beginning and the end. Self-control is here necessary. If a feeling steals in such as discontent, discouragement, reluctance, or others, (I am not speaking here about envy and disloyalty and other such feelings which kill the life of God) it is necessary, at once, to realise what it is that I have put into my own heart, where God lives, and whether it is possible for the Mother Most Holy to take hold of such a heart in her own Most Chaste Hands, and to offer it to God. The world calls this interior practice, or the culture of feelings, but this is the Christian impetus of the soul to God, as the final goal. This is the right and obligation of each Christian, who has to live by faith.

In the Rosary, pondering on the feelings of the Heart of the Mother Most Holy is the most perfect nursery for simpletons, as also an academy for philosophers. The Immaculate Heart of Mary is the true reflection of the virtues and feelings of the Sacred Heart of the Saviour. Let you ask her in the Rosary that you, also, would be formed in the model of the Divine Heart of Jesus, and through this you will be most perfectly united with her Immaculate Heart. And then, in spite of your falls, and rising from them with sorrow, in spite of your extreme poverty and sins, God will look on you with delight, seeing, even though it would be microscopically, the reflection in your hearts of the Most Holy Hearts of Jesus and Mary.

"LEARN FROM ME, THAT I AM GENTLE AND HUMBLE OF HEART". Mary Most Holy learnt this most perfectly, and you also she will teach and instruct through the Rosary and in the Rosary. Amen.

The SECRET POWER of the ROSARY

THE PRAYER TO THE ANGEL
FOR THE OPENING OF THE FLOODGATES OF GRACE
OF THE IMMACULATE HEART OF MARY

Mother of Divine Grace, Mother of Mercy, Mother weeping over Her children! In Your Immaculate Heart the Lord deposited all the graces necessary for us. Pour them, we humbly beseech thee, on

- sinners
- those who do not ask for them and who do not wish to accept them – but receive them,
- prisoners and the persecuted, who might surrender to the temptation of despair,
- the powerless and unknowing who are threatened with doubt,
- the frightened and little hearts who are threatened with apostasy,
- the proud and blind who are threatened with error and the leading of others into wrong ways,
- the suffering and distressed who do not know where to look for ease and rescue,
- the ardent, the faithful, those who love You, those who are threatened with danger on every side,
- those torn away from God through violence on account of the scandal of those who are ignorant of the fact that they are children of God and do not yearn for You,

- those who are to be killed, but do not know the hour or the moment,
- those who hope for everything from You and through You, because they, in their heart, are united with You in the Slavery of Love,
- those burning in the flames of cleansing pain, longing for You, and for the moment of which they are already certain,
- this, our nation, whose Queen You have been, are, and will be: Queen of Poland,
- those nations, who with the hearts of best sons and daughters, love and adore You,
- those nations who have renounced You, their own Mother,
- those poor people who do not know that You are also their Mother, and on the Pope, and all the Orders, and all who have the sacrament of Holy Orders and who have given their life to God in service. O Lord! Upon these deign to pour out your most generous graces, because they have been, and now are, most awfully hated, tormented and brought to ruin by the foe.

Mary, we beseech you unceasingly for this. Let every beat of our hearts knock on Your Heart of Gold, opening It to the outpouring of these graces on everyone, everyone!

Through the love and delight of the Most Holy Trinity, through the love of the Divine Heart of your Son, through the love and adoration of all the Angels, through the love of all the hearts of the people, who were, who are, and always will be, the prizes you have earned through the love of your Maternal Immaculate Heart, we implore You to hear us, because we trust – we trust so much that our trust cannot be disappointed. And so, in peace and love, our hearts with every beat desire to sing to You, O Lord Most Wonderful, the Magnificat of thanksgiving, both now and forever. Amen.

SUPPLEMENT

"I need souls who would be in the hands of Mary."

(Extracts from the diary of a certain Priest).

For the last times the Lord Jesus has reserved the outpouring of mercy for those who will be for the one named: Mary. Through this the Lord Jesus wishes to assign, so to speak, the compulsion of his Justice. "I open to her the entire abyss of Mercy." In the presence of the miracles of Mercy, which will be worked then through Mary, everything hitherto in existence will be turned pale. For this reason the Lord Jesus gives Mary special power of consolation of His Heart, through winning souls for Him and teaching them true love of God, and He wishes to reward her for the fact that in the time of His suffering She united so completely with His desire of suffering, that forgetting about Her own feelings, she did nothing, such as Veronica did, to console Him. Mary cannot love God love more than she already loves Him, but to some extent she augments it through the souls who give themselves to Her. We have to give ourselves in the slavery of love of Mary for Jesus).

Those who devote themselves to Mary, who are really owned by Mary, will become the spirit of Her Love. They will love God, as Mary does – not to the degree of Her Love, because this is reserved for Her, and nobody will be able to the same degree as Mary, but it will be of the same nature as Her Love.

"I am very anxious to see how My Will, in which I have put all My Love, is a delight for people. But I experience so little of this from people. They do not wish to give me the joy of seeing that My Will is their delight. They do not wish to see and acknowledge My Love in it, and this Mary would teach them."

The truth about the mediation of Mary, which has to be confirmed in the Church, cannot possibly be suspended in a void, but it must be alive in souls. There are souls who are alive to this truth. But still so few are taking it to heart. This matter is most dear to the Heart of the Lord Jesus. It embraces everything else.

In the approaching times souls not joined to Mary will be subject to singular peril on account of the intensive activities of satan. Simultaneously will come an intensification of the works of Mary. God has conferred on Her such power that, through the force of its supplication and action, it will call to mind the omnipotence of God.

(Like Jesus, Who often first heals the bodies and then the souls, so also Mary, in the last times, through many miracles of healing will draw to Herself the souls of the people. But yet a time draws near when Mary will be working first of all in the souls of people. If it is said that the Kingdom of God is within us, so also the activities of Mary, which must prepare for this Kingdom, must be within us).

"I expect you in particular to help Me in the bringing about of My designs."

The Lord Jesus promised that following the complete giving of self to Mary there ensues a revival and flowering of the Community. Each resurrected one has to live in Mary, and Mary has to live in each resurrected one. "Let yourselves be the glory and triumph of Mary."

We are the favorites of Jesus. We have in a particular way the fullness of His Truth. "Mary lays claim to Her right in your Community, and I am not able to refuse Her anything."

It is possible to compare the truth about the life of Mary in souls to the parable about the treasure buried in the soil. Our Community possesses it, but it has not yet become fully productive; we do not fully use it; we do not even share it with others.

***

January, 1948.

The chief emphasis must be laid on the Love of the Heart of Jesus for Mary. This Heart loves Her so much that it aches. Jesus wants us to share in the pangs of His Heart loving Mary.

If we wish to be members of Jesus Christ, all the manifestations of His life must be in us. His Love for Mary must be in us.

We must be intermediaries of the Love of Jesus for Mary. Jesus desires to love Mary in us. Jesus demands love for His Heart loving Mary. We must especially adore Jesus in His Love for Mary. Jesus desires that we would be devoted to this Love.

The SECRET POWER of the ROSARY

When we have in ourselves a place for the Love of Jesus for Mary, when loving Mary together with Jesus, we will wish to fulfill His Desires, and then necessarily, and as a consequence, Mary comes to us with Her Love of Jesus.

We must calculate from this that if we are desirous to console the Heart of Jesus Loving Mary, if we are desirous to bring about relief to Jesus in His suffering which He experiences looking always at the tears in the Eyes of His Most Beloved Mother, then through this we will be entirely devoted to Her desire that Jesus would be loved, and then Mary utilizes this devotion of ours in complete fullness. She takes everything that is ours, and in return she gives everything that is hers – which is that for which She solely lives – Jesus and Her chaste love for Him. Her desire that Jesus would be loved is poured into our hearts, and She directs our entire existence to this one purpose. By this means, in us and through us, all the desires of the Heart of Jesus will be fulfilled.

Every time Jesus turns to Mary asking: "What do you desire?" He receives, always, only one answer: "Son that You would be loved." Here begins the suffering of His Heart. Jesus Who is the All-Powerful God is not able to fulfill the desire of His Most Beloved Mother. He is the poorest of sons, because He is the most loving and the most powerless if we do not come to Him with help. Without us Jesus is unable to fulfill the desire of Mary, and for this reason He desires to manifest His Love for Mary and Her suffering, so that we would move and bow to the existence of this Love.

In Fatima, Mary, who in general never speaks about herself, still said: "MY SON DESIRES THAT I WOULD

171

BE MORE LOVED." In the name of Jesus Mary demanded love for herself. Whoever loves Her will love what she desires: THAT JESUS WOULD BE LOVED.

Is there someone among us who would be able to say that this wish announced at Fatima by the lips of Mary is not directed to him? If there were such a one, this would be a soul who already loved God with chaste, perfect love. And since there is not such a person, how have we reacted to this wish? Have we fulfilled it, and are we trying to continue to fulfill it? Because it is not possible to put any limits here.

Have I already given Mary everything – in the full sense of this word – so that She could have it at Her disposal for the desire of Her love for Jesus? And if not what is withholding me? Is it not necessary to attach this call to the words, which we repeat daily in the Office: "Oh! That today you would listen to His voice, harden not your hearts."

Jesus desiring to reveal Himself as the Son of Mary, desiring to reveal His Own Love of Mary wishes to strike a chord of deepest tenderness in the heart of humanity. Each one of us has a mother, and we know what love of Mother is. If at sometime we were compelled to look helplessly on her suffering, the thought of Jesus would be the singular relief given to us. All our hope would be in Him, and likewise the Heart of Jesus, in His Own love for Mary, puts His complete hope in us.

Mary in Fatima did not say that God, or Jesus, wishes that She would be more loved, but in accordance with His wish She signified distinctly: "My Son wishes that

The SECRET POWER of the ROSARY

I would be more loved". If we refuse, to whom will Jesus go?

Let tomorrow, the First Friday, be a day of joy for the Heart of Jesus loving Mary. Let Jesus know that among us, hearts are preparing for the reception of this Love; for the sharing of it with Him; prepared for the service of Her desires. Let it be, that thanks to us, tomorrow Jesus will not see tears in the eyes of Mary. Tomorrow let Mary find scores of warm hearts, which burn with Love taken directly from the Heart of Jesus, for the reception of Her love for Jesus.

If we would surrender ourselves, wishing to serve the desires of the Love of Jesus for Mary, we would certainly turn principally towards Her. But at this time what is the position? Behold, desiring to console Her we must love Jesus; desiring to adore Her, we must in ourselves repeat Her Love of Jesus; desiring to recompense the pain in Her Heart, we must love Jesus on behalf of those who do not love Him. Desiring truly to love her alone we must constantly, together with her, fulfill her will which is transmitted to us in the words: "Do everything whatsoever He recommends to you."

This, only, is the most chaste, the most splendid love of God (…"whoever does the Will of My Father is the one who loves Me…") then devotion to the Desires of the Love of Jesus for Mary, leads to the fulfillment in us of all the desires of God.

Do not let Jesus feel that among us there is a non-appreciation of His Love for Mary. As, more and more, He exposes to us the depth of His Heart; let it not be in vain. Let us penetrate the mystery of the Love of Jesus for Mary, and when we take possession of this Love in our hearts, let us remember that it is unlimited.

We wish to understand what it means to be between these two Loves: the Love of Jesus for Mary, and then in the aftermath of this, Mary's Love for Jesus. Does truly loving Jesus not oblige us to make a joyful consciousness of the fact that we can heal the painful injuries of His Heart by bringing about (in our hearts) His love for Mary? Can we now leave Jesus alone in what He experiences and suffers in His Love for Mary, more so now that we know that only we have the power to relieve Him?

We must not let go from our hands the power of delighting Jesus. Let us absorb ourselves in the Heart of Jesus Loving Mary, particularly at that time when he comes to us in Holy Communion, when we have His living Heart in ourselves. Let us give our whole heart to the disposition of Jesus, so that it will be able to fill Mary with His Love. And this Love is unlimited; therefore, we can never say, "This is enough". We must also be insatiable in our desire of service to this Love.

Let us remember that if we accept in ourselves Jesus loving Mary, Jesus will not wish, even for a moment, to disunite us from Mary. Always, These Two Loves through our hearts will overflow. Out of love for Jesus, through giving His Love to Mary, we will be doing only that which Mary desires; we will love Jesus through fulfillment of His Will, only not alone, but with Her Love, which advanced to heroism.

Can we perhaps imagine to ourselves the gratitude of Jesus to those who devote themselves to His love for Mary in complete offering; those to whom the satisfaction of the desires of this Love becomes their singular concern, singular need, and the greatest joy?

Let us not permit for a moment that the Heart of Jesus would be shuddering from apprehension that through entrusting to us this mystery of His Love for Mary, He would meet, from our side, with indifference and disrespect.

****

7ᵗʰ May, 1948.

Jesus wishes to manifest much more about His Love for Mary, inasmuch as Her life on earth was hidden.

The responsibility of souls who in themselves are giving a place Jesus Loving Mary: – It would be cruel to deprive Jesus, even for a moment, of the company of Mary. Nobody has an idea of the strength and power they have if they offer requests to Jesus in the name of His Love for Mary. For Jesus, it is like the Smile of Mary.

Souls desiring to serve the Love of Jesus for Mary can count on a quick unification with Him; this is a very strong temptation for Jesus; Jesus desires that the coming of the Kingdom of Mary would be as a result of His Love for Her. This prayer (Koronka) is a caressing of the Love of Jesus for Mary, and of Mary for Jesus.

Jesus desires to love Mary in all His Mystical Body, and because He made Her Queen of His Heart, Mary must also be Queen of our hearts. Then, like a genuine Queen, Mary will be governing our hearts, making Her demands of them, so that they would love Jesus. Mary is a very demanding Queen; all of the power of the love of our hearts She directs to Jesus. Preparing this Her Kingdom, that is to say, our hearts, according to His likeness, and taking away everything opposing that same demand, She gives them completely to Jesus, in accordance with the imparting to us of these words: "Do everything, whatsoever He recommends to you," and in this way teaching them of never-ending, incessant love of fulfillment of the Will of God in the closest union with Her, and giving everything possible to this needed help of Grace.

Having to Her disposition the entire Heart of Jesus, She becomes for us, truly, Mediatrix of Graces. This is why Holy Church combines the feast of Mary Mediatrix of Graces and Queen of the Heart of Jesus. The dogma of the Universal Mediation of Mary must be sealed with the mutual Love of Jesus and Mary.

Mary sang the Magnificat when through Her the first miracle of Grace took place.

The manifestation of the Love of Jesus for Mary is for strong, stimulated souls, who would be coming into closest unity with Her, and permitting Her to fulfill Her role as Mediatrix of Graces. The Love of Mary for Jesus is the most perfect reflection of the Love of Jesus for the Eternal Father. As the will of the Father was the only nourishment for Jesus, so Mary lives only on the will of Jesus. The manifestation of the love of Jesus for Mary, in its final purpose, aims only at this: that the will of God would be perfectly fulfilled. As we cherish, with greatest veneration, the smallest fragment of the Eucharist, likewise must we also observe the least of the manifestations of the Will of God. As Mary reflects the Most Perfect Love of Jesus for the Eternal Father, so we must reflect the most perfect Love of Mary for Jesus.

God the Father, Jesus, Mary and we ourselves, are one chain of Love in the Holy Spirit.

****

24th May, 1948.

Through giving ourselves completely to Mary, we delight Her, because, in ourselves, we are giving to Her the opportunity of living again for God, of suffering for the salvation of souls and of growing in love, which now for Her is no longer possible. The soul who truly serves the desires of the Love of Jesus for Mary, immediately finds a place for his own "Yes". It becomes only a form, in which Jesus and Mary live. Jesus makes use of it in the love of Mary; Mary makes use of it in the love of Jesus.

Mary is Herself the first offering of the Love of Jesus for Her. Knowing about the desires of the Love of Jesus for Her, and about Her Own prerogative of Mediatrix of Graces, She Herself co-operates with the soul which Jesus chooses as an offering of His Love for Her, so that completely united with Her, it should become what Jesus desires – a constant consolation of Her Heart, with a field for free operation for the salvation of souls.

Only the Holy Spirit can accomplish in us the desires of the Love of Jesus for Mary. This has to be entirely His work. He follows closely behind Mary everywhere she goes. She allures Him to the souls in which she lives. The more a soul is devoted to Mary, the fuller it possesses the

Holy Spirit. The soul united to Mary becomes possessed by Him in an unspeakable way. It becomes for Him a second Mary, which helps in the work of salvation of souls.

For Mary – so inconceivably beloved of the Holy Trinity – it is not sufficient for Her to repay with just the Love of Her Own Heart; She desires, furthermore, to love God with our hearts. The prerogative of Mediatrix enables Her to have the realization of this desire. Souls committed to the desires of the Love of Jesus for Mary become, through the mediation of Mary, drawn into the plan of works of the entire Holy Trinity. Do not forget what the love of Mary was like: The simplicity of the fulfillment of the Will of God. And in this is Contemplation of God. In the Love of the Holy Trinity the Heart of Jesus, Son of Mary, is on fire with love for Mary.

The giving of oneself to Mary is the beginning of a spiritual death. That which never existed in Her, at the moment of Her coming into us, must become silent in us. Mary brings Jesus with Her. We must make a place for Him; otherwise, once again Mary would have to withdraw. Mary did not despise the stable, even though it was so miserable; it sufficed that it was empty. Jesus desires, that in loving Mary, we would be joined with the Love of His Heart for Her, so that we would be as springs drawn out from Her, and that on our part this would be a conscious act.

Hidden in this wonderful mystery is growth in love for Jesus. Because the Love of Jesus for Mary in us leads us to a closer union with Her, and we discover the consequence of this under the unceasing action of the Holy Spirit which, controlling us, gradually leads us, more and more in the life of love of the Entire Holy Trinity. To be drawn into the life of the Holy Trinity means – to live with Her Love in the spreading of this Love to all souls. This leads to the giving of the soul, which is received into Her hands as an offering for the Love of oneself to the Love of Jesus for Mary is sentenced to death; death to everything, which is not serving the desires of Mary that Jesus, would be loved.

What bliss for Mary is such a soul! The desire that Jesus would be loved is realized first of all in Her, in an unspeakable way, and through it, in other souls. There remains, however, the possibility of unfaithfulness. Therefore, there is a necessity of prayer to the Holy Spirit.

The soul committed to the Love of Jesus for Mary, and to the serving of Her through fulfillment of Her desires, comes more and more into a consciousness that it, itself, no longer lives, but that Mary has occupied its place. Through daily fulfillment of the Will of God the soul continually yields a place to Her, loses itself in Her and begins to live the new life of the Love of Mary for Jesus, which is brought about by the Holy Spirit. He instructs and develops this life committed to Her. The soul following in the footsteps of Mary He takes as His prisoner, in its entirety.

****

29th May, 1948:

The Will of God is the continuous outpouring upon us of the Love of God. God keeps us in loving embrace with His Own Will. Every expression of It is a declaration of the Love of Jesus. Each Divine "I desire" is an expression of His love. With this Love, which we constantly meet, we can continuously unite. God loves me with each expression of His Will. Through uniting with It, I am plunging into the same Divine Heart.

Mary, in this devotion to the Will of God, in other words to His Love, went so far as to become Queen of His Heart. God so trusted Her that He left This Heart to Her disposition.

At each "I love God in His Will", I am to put my "I love" into effect through fulfillment of His Will.

Demanding us to do this and only this, which Jesus desires, continually, Mary is immersing us constantly in His Love and in His Heart. Perpetual motion continues always from Jesus to Mary, and from Mary to Jesus, and again anew, until the measure of the desires of Jesus is fulfilled. The concrete result of devotion to the Heart of Jesus, in other words, to His love, is a perfect realization that His Will is the expression of His Love.

When we have offered all our actions to Mary, she in turn then offers them to God for the salvation of sinners. Then all His Love radiates, and God gives grace for the measure of Mary's love, not ours. Jesus desires to entrust His Love of Mary to our Congregation. He desires to have a place from which this, His Love, would specifically radiate.

The most precious pearls of our souls are these three qualifications: "I am nothing." "I have nothing." "I cannot do anything." They enable Jesus to apply in us the full exquisiteness of His Love. They soothe His desires to give. They open the field of Mary's action. The Act of Consecration to the Immaculate Heart of Mary contributed to the fact that Jesus so trusted us.

The SECRET POWER of the ROSARY

"Behold I have merged you into the desires of My Heart." On how we receive Jesus, desiring to confide His Love of Mary to us, depends whether or not Jesus will be able to go further along this way. Jesus desires that we would be the first to respond to the call of His Heart. Through our hearts He wishes to pave the way for others. Only when, in us, He lives in fullness with His Love for Mary, will Jesus be able to go further. "Let you desire this fullness, if you love Me and souls."

Jesus desires and expects prayer. It will be evidence of the fact that the desires of His Love for His Mother have become our desires. "Upon your acceptance of this matter depends its further progress."

Because a cross must precede the realization of the desires of the Love of Jesus for Mary, this great love for the Heart of Jesus Loving Mary is, therefore, indispensable in order that such a death on the cross to bring about the fulfillment of His desires would be possible. The truth about the wheat grain has to be applied here.

Our devotion to Mary must be, in the full sense of the word, absolute; otherwise the saying about "complete trust" would not have a genuine basis. When one gives to Mary the most complete freedom of action, only then can the most complete trust have a place. Through the manifestation of His love for Mary, Jesus gives into our hands power over His Own Heart.

In connection with the revelations in Fatima. "Behold and tell of this which, I am likely to do in order to console the Heart of My Mother. Do you wish to participate in this consolation? For this, to love My Heart Loving Mary, you must love Me very much.

"Behold, the beginning of the revelation of My Love For Mary was ('My Son desires that I would be more loved').

"See to what extremes I go for sinners. – What am I not ready to do for My Mother? Write ... that I am ready for the greatest miracles in order to show that which, for so long, I have kept in My Heart for the last times.

"Here it is not possible to have limits, because My Love for Mary is infinite.

"I knew where I have to turn" (the spirit of the Congregation; the life of Jesus in us and, therefore, also His Love for Mary).

"What words must I still have to convince you?" (Of the mystery of His Love for Mary. Jesus yearns to this moment).

"I have loved your Congregation with very great love. All the hope of My Heart loving Mary, I have placed in you".

Jesus gives every soul individual penetration in the truth of His Love for Mary. For the time being, the song of this Love is sung by two voices. Jesus waits for the rise of a many-voiced choir. He desires that this choir would be blended (with the Fathers). The conductor of this choir will be the Holy Spirit Himself.

Jesus wishes to overpower us with His Own Love for Mary. We will be the paradise of His Heart loving Mary. – "I am giving you the most precious jewel of My Heart". If Jesus, in a special way, manifested His Love for people, how much more deserving of this is the Love of His Heart for Mary.

The SECRET POWER of the ROSARY

On tomorrow's day we must receive Jesus loving Mary, so to say, in the name of the entire Congregation. Jesus, tomorrow wishes to experience in us a twofold joy: firstly, from the Birth of Mary, and secondly, when through our acceptance, it becomes openly accepted by the entire Congregation. He already consoles His Mother with the assurance that there are, at our place, souls prepared to serve the desires of Their Mutual Love, although they do not know yet what awaits them. Mary, tomorrow, must be accepted by us with the Love of Jesus. The first Birth of Mary was hidden.

Now, Jesus desires to manifest and to experience in us, and through us, the joy of the Son of Mary's Own Heart greeting His Mother.

****

8th September, 1948.

Jesus entrusts to us, not only His Love for Mary, but also Mary Herself. He waited purposely for the day of Her Birth, so that He would be giving the Little Her to us, to stress that He desires that Her Own Love for Him would grow in us. Accepting the tiny Mary, we must wrap Her in the Love of Jesus for Her.

Jesus relies very much on this, that we would understand well what this means to Him. In the revelation of the Love of Jesus for Mary, the central point rests, not on Mary but on the Heart of Jesus, Son of Mary, on the Heart of Jesus Loving Mary.

There is another want, which Jesus feels in His Mystical Body. It is true that Mary is loved in Him, even very much, but there is not sufficient consciousness, that depending on how much we truly love Mary, so much do we permit Jesus to love Her in us. If Jesus gave us Mary for our Mother, He did this first of all, out of Love for Her, in order to satisfy Her desire to pour into our hearts love for Him, and only in the second place, out of love for us. Consequently, we also in our attitude to Mary, must give first place to the love of Jesus for Mary, to acknowledge It as the only source of animating our hearts with love for Her.

Jesus hungers and thirsts for the life with love of Mary, in us. He desires to be well known and adored in this Love. He desires that we would acknowledge that if it were not for this love, we would not have Mary nor all that She is for our souls, their salvation and sanctification. Only on the condition that we receive to our hearts the Love of Jesus for Mary are we able to satisfy Her desires of ownership of us for Jesus.

In the Mystical Body of Jesus the repetition and prolongation of His life on earth is accomplished. Jesus gave Himself in offering for the salvation of souls, not directly, but as the Son of Mary, through Her. In this capacity He still lives in the members of His Mystical Body. Jesus stressed this, when in the moment of the accomplishment of His Sacrifice, He said to Mary: "Woman, behold Thy son".

Mary has only one Son: Jesus, Who Himself became the Sacrifice for the sins of the world. Everyone who wishes to be the son of Mary will be with Him in the measure of a repetition in himself of Jesus, an offering for the salvation of souls. At the same time He confirms this truth about the role of Mary as Mediatrix of Graces, inasmuch as Jesus, desiring to satisfy Her greatest desire that He would be loved, constantly gives Himself to Her in His members, Her sons, as a continuous offering for the salvation of souls. The desire of the Cross is, therefore, the most powerful expression of our love for Mary.

****

12th September, 1948.

"Do you realize from this matter that you have in your own hands deliverance for the whole world?"

This prayer ('Koronka'), Crown, must enfold the whole world with fire; it causes people to be burning with love for Jesus. "It brings about this power of Mary's Love for Me and the power of My Love for Mary". Jesus shows me His Love in order that I would behave likewise to the souls that are placed on my way, in accordance with the time when these words were said: "You must be for them such as I am for you". He gives me to understand that my devotion for Him, should arouse in me the desire to give to Him souls with prayer, sacrifice, and love. Jesus desires, in me, to show to the whole world, how to love the souls that are turning towards Him.

When it appeared to me that Jesus oversteps the bounds in His Kindness, I said only: "Jesus, what are You doing?" – "I love souls; I love them to folly. Do not fear. I watch over the work of My Love, not lamenting of anything, in order that it would be realized."

As a mother, before she gives her child to the world, gathers in the heart treasures of love for him, so also, I have to prepare, in order to become in spirit, a mother for souls. In advance, I have to embrace with warm love all those whom Jesus has placed on my path. Jesus reminded me once, the spoken words that He is almost jealous of me, having immediate contact with souls. Jesus delights in the thought of the nearness of souls, through me. When I expressed my surprise and questioned whether it was not much better to work directly, e.g. in the Tabernacle, Jesus replied, sorrowfully, that not everybody comes to Him there, or – although they are coming – they have little faith and do not wish to listen to His Voice. Many a time He has greater possibilities of action through the members of His "Mystical Body". Anyway, this is the means of which, from the beginning, He frequently makes use. Therefore, He told me once that in me, He wishes to be bread, nourishment, and Communion for others.

Jesus said that He finds joy in the mutual outpouring of love for Him, among us. The offering of the Love of Jesus for Mary will not be judged. It is Jesus Who has to judge – His Own Love for Mary or Mary's Love for Him. In thanksgiving for the rendering of good deeds to Her, Mary not only diminishes all the sins of souls, but from them She draws still much more good, through humiliation, sorrow, and great love.

As an earthly mother gives birth to her child amid great pain, yet she experiences a certain happiness in giving life to him – likewise Mary experienced certain feelings of happiness in the spiritual sense, when standing under the Cross She heard the words: "Woman, behold Thy Son"

The SECRET POWER of the ROSARY

Clasping, in spirit, to Her Heart all Her children, represented by St. John, Mary, with all Her Being, seems to turn towards those who are in the death of the spirit. Her Heart sinks in pain at the thought of their loss. The Hearts of Jesus and Mary feel in unison: "Father forgive them for they know not what they do." Jesus and Mary desire the moment of His Passion to be prolonged to the end of the world, in order to save them. This goes on in the members of the Mystical Body of Jesus in the Church.

To love Jesus and Mary – is to give oneself in sacrifice for souls. Jesus, confiding to the Congregation, through me, His Heart Loving Mary, desired to preserve the tradition of His Resurrection. He made the same gesture as He did at the time of the first appearance to Mary Magdalene.

We must be mediators of the Love of Jesus for Mary, through most frequent spiritual Holy Communions, and in one's own heart giving Him to Mary, to satisfy in this way the desires of His Love for Her.

He waits for me in complete impoverishment. Using me Jesus and Mary will outdo one another in the desires of the fulfillment of Their Mutual Love. In the moment of Holy Vows to find oneself in the Hands of Mary, as Jesus was in the moment of the Presentation in the Temple, and at the same time to be Jesus for Mary, who in this moment receives confirmation of Her participation in His Holocaustic Sacrifice. As an offering of Their Mutual Love, to repeat in oneself the dedication of Mary to Jesus, and the dedication of Jesus to Mary. Dedicated to Mary with the Love of Jesus, I am experiencing in myself a repetition of His offering in the same way as it was repeated in Mary. The moment of Holy Vows – is the beginning. The end is "only the remaining of Jesus on the Cross, and Mary under the Cross. Mary preserves and leads Her second Jesus to Calvary where again, it will be Jesus on the Cross and Mary under the Cross, and actually, the most perfect repetitions are only with Jesus in Mary.

The present rules of the Immaculate Heart of Mary:

"In My anger and justice, I will be continually yielding to Her. I am compelled to this, through My Love for Mary. But I desire that the world would know to whom, and why, it is indebted for My Mercy."

"The one who will be an apostle of My Love for Mary – will, in himself, be a picture of this, which he himself will be announcing in My Name."

The repetition in self of Mary, and of Her faithful heroism and such direct and extraordinary deprivation, of great love growing from moment to moment, but not by outward deed, is extraordinary. Only in one point, in the repetition of self of Mary, (it would be possible) to exceed the bounds – in the Sacrifice. The union of my soul with Jesus has to be a repetition of the union of Mary with Jesus. On the day of Holy Vows Jesus wishes to see before Himself – His Own Mother. Jesus gives to me the right of handling Him, as His Mother. As in the stable at Bethlehem, everything was recompensed to Jesus in the Loving Arms of His Mother, so it must be in my soul – in every moment to deal with Jesus as Mary did, continual conformity with Him in His Most Holy Will, and faithfulness in tiny things. An inspiration would be to ask for admission rather of everything, than of one conscious and voluntary disloyalty. Jesus does not wish to sense in me anyone other than His Most Holy Mother. – "Only Mary can rescue the misery of your soul."

"To the seriously ill one calls the renowned doctor. – Do you know what it means to be My Mother?" (The sword of grief).

At each moment I might again become Judas.

"I, your God, Who at this moment speaks in your soul, do not guarantee to you that your salvation is certain".

Each infidelity shatters the bonds of the slavery of love. The offering of love of Jesus for Mary must have in itself Their love of souls.

The treasures of Jesus and Mary:

My lot will be like the Cross of Jesus, and like the sword of Mary.

A warning for excessive self-certainty – the threat of admittance to the fall of St. Peter:

Jesus said that He never worked miracles of grace through the great and the proud. For this it is necessary to be very little and very humble. The most humble is The Mediatrix of All Graces. Humility delights Jesus, He finds His bliss in it and then the beams of His Love are closely touching my soul. The conditions for the fulfillment of the desires of the Love of Jesus for Mary are in my hand – the constant desire of prayer.

"You are a beloved child of the Holy Trinity, because the entire Holy Trinity finds bliss in the communion in your soul with Mary."

Announcement of the particular works of the Holy Spirit: He brings in the fire of Love, which I desire.

Pray with greater faith, hope and love. This is necessary to fulfill what Jesus requires from the Church. Jesus wishes to show such Mercy, which up to now was not shown because He did not reveal until now, His Love for Mary.

At the expressed doubt that probably the greatest charity was the Redemption, whereas the greatest is His Love for the Father, Jesus did not deny, but elucidated that in the face of the waste of Graces and of the Fruits of the Redemption, the present Mercy seems to be still greater. The Love of Jesus for Mary is "a component" of His Love for the Father; it is its concrete expression. In order to fulfill the Will of the Father, Jesus, out of Love for Him, became the Son of Mary. Mary continually remembers the reciprocal love of the Three Persons of the Holy Trinity. From here, Her completely devoted soul draws down on Itself the special Love of the Entire Holy Trinity.

I became named the beggar-woman-bride. I do not cease to be this, immediately from the moment of Holy Vows. Jesus will be obliged to be suffering with me for a long time still. In the participation now of the particular protection of the Holy Spirit's Own Love for Mary, Jesus will not be able to give less than the Holy Spirit Himself, because Jesus loves Him. For this – in order that I would be really in the "same Heart of the Mother of the Church" with the Love of Jesus for Mary, I must be particularly espoused to the Holy Spirit. On the day of Holy Vows, transformed in love, I will be clothed in the garment of shining faith, with white chastity; I will draw near to Jesus with trust and faith in His Love, and all this will evidence of humility, without which nothing of this would be possible to obtain. My life must be known, so that nobody would be afraid to draw near to the mystery of the Love of Jesus and Mary but that it would be seen that it is Mercy, of such a kind that never yet has been. Every least anxiety about the future is an offense against the love of Jesus and a denial of the reality of the slavery of Mary – from love.

After the showing of my extreme poverty, Jesus said that with such He regards me as a beggar woman. He desires now only humility and devotion. He loves His Own Eternal Thought in me, this picture He has before His Eyes. Beginning, together with Him, to go the way, will shape not only me, but also other souls, because I have given everything to Mary. For this reason Jesus loves me so very much. I will be thinking that I am becoming worse and worse, and meanwhile, I will be only seeing more clearly. If I will struggle, these miseries will not be an absolute hindrance to Jesus, in order that through me He would pour into other souls love for Himself. I will be only seeing well, that everything is His – and not my activity. – When I asked Jesus whether He did not withdraw in the presence of my disbeliefs, He replied: "I desire to receive your poverty in security for My Love. I never give it back if you do not repay My Love".

I have to be united with the Heart of Jesus, in particular in His humility and gentleness, as well as His Love for Mary. I have to know only one voice; there has to be only one song in my soul: "May the Heart of Jesus Loving Mary – be loved!" Everything else must lapse into silence. In the temple of the Love of Jesus for Mary – there has to be silence.

At the time of recollection, the introduction to the Heart of Jesus there where Mary Most Magnificently reigns: Jesus wished through this to show how delightful to

Him is my devotion to Mary. He brought me there, where I find unity with Mary in the highest degree. Mary is Queen of the Heart of Jesus, first of all, though humility and love. Humility and Love are also the chief characteristics of the Heart of Jesus. The Love of Jesus addresses itself, first of all, to Mary and then to souls (for that matter, to creation).

And behold, my whole world, apart from this I do not have to know anything else. Jesus, Mary, and souls, and saying – Jesus – I can likewise say – Most Holy Trinity. God so loved the world that He gave His Only Son. He gave Him to Mary, at the instance of the Holy Spirit.

In the name of Mary is conceived the fullest mystery of the Love of the Most Holy Trinity for souls, the mystery of the Incarnation. I am in the Heart of Jesus, Son of Mary, in the Heart of Jesus Loving Mary. The measure of my devotion has to be the measure of the Love of Jesus for Mary; the measure of His desire would be that in me He would again be crucified for the salvation of those over whom Mary weeps. Jesus chose me in order to give Mary this greater joy, because I am from those over whom Mary was weeping, but who have been redeemed, and from whom, now, Jesus and Mary can expect love and devotion so much greater, inasmuch as a greater debt to me was pardoned. I will be as proof to the miracle of the Graces, such as the Heart of Jesus Loving Mary desires to effect.

Jesus wished that I would see the struggle of satan for souls, in order that I would hear these words: "TWO HEARTS HAVE CONQUERED ME!" This is the manifestation of the Power of the Mutual Love of Jesus and Mary. In consciousness and faith in this power, I have to stand up to the struggle with satan. This prayer: "May the Heart of Jesus Loving Mary be loved!" has to be my breathing, and the beating of my heart. With satan I have to struggle, first of all through humility, and later through prayer and sacrifice. Not one moment without suffering; not one day without humiliation. In order that I would fulfill this, I must live with this with which These Two Hearts live.

"Your life is only in the Love of Jesus for Mary".

Thus far the Heart of Jesus and the Heart of Mary have been revealed, but this is still not everything. Now the time has come for the revelation of the mutual love of These Two Hearts, and this will only be the fulfillment of all the thoughts of God, as it were, the crowning of these two revelations.

These words: "TWO HEARTS HAVE CONQUERED ME" – satan will be obliged to express at the end of the struggle which he wages with God. They, at the same time, will fulfill the announcement given by God in Paradise: "I am placing enmity between thee and The Woman, between thy progeny and Her seed." – Already, in this announcement was contained the mystery of the Love of Jesus for Mary. Mary, out of Love for Jesus, saves souls, and She does this with the power of all graces, which, out of love for Her, the Heart of Her Son leaves to Her disposal.

The powerful cause, which leads me to death from love, through the fulfillment of Holy Vows, will be the Love of Jesus for Mary.

****

2nd February, 1949.

PRAYERS

The SECRET POWER of the ROSARY

Come O Holy Spirit
Come by means of the
powerful intercession
of the Immaculate Heart of Mary,
Your Well-Beloved Spouse.

Jesus, Mary and Joseph - I love You very much.
I beg You to spare the life of the pre-born child
that I have spiritually adopted, and who is in
danger of abortion.

Prayer for Protection

+In the Name of the Most Blessed Trinity,
of God the Almighty Father,
of the Only Begotten Son,
of the Glorious Holy Spirit
Depart evil spirits, so that
you may not see nor hear our works and plans;
that you shall not deceive, nor persecute us,
nor interfere, nor cause confusion
in our endeavors to serve God!

The Lord our God, Who is also your Lord,
COMMANDS you to be gone
and never to return! Amen.

Oh Most Holy and Almighty Father,
make us invisible to our enemies. Amen.

BARBARA KLOSS

****

Holy Spirit Inspire us.
Love of God, Absorb us.
Mary Mother, Look at us.
On the Right Way, Guide us.
With Jesus, Bless us.
From all dangers,
from all Illusions,
from all Malice,
save us. Amen.

[Above prayer dictated by Holy Spirit
to Mary of Jesus Crucified,
a Carmelite nun in Bethlehem;
blessed by Holy Father.]

Queen of Heaven

August Queen of heaven, sovereign Mistress of the Angels,
who did receive from the beginning the mission and power
to crush the serpent's head.
We beseech Thee to send Thy holy angels,
that under Thy command and by Thy power
they may pursue the evil spirits,
encounter them on every side, resist their bold attacks,
and drive them hence into the abyss of woe.
Most Holy Mother, send Thy angels to defend us
and to drive the cruel enemy from us.
All holy Angels and Archangels, help and defend us.

The SECRET POWER of the ROSARY

O good and tender Mother!
Thou shall ever be our Love and Hope.
Holy Angels and Archangels, keep and defend us. Amen.

Holy Father St. Joseph, guardian of virgins, to whose faithful custody, Christ Jesus, Innocence Itself, and Mary, Virgin of Virgins, were committed; I pray and beseech you, by these dear pledges, Jesus and Mary, that being preserved from all uncleanness, I may with spotless mind, pure heart, and chaste body, ever serve Jesus and Mary most chastely all the days of my life. <u>Amen</u>.

Jesus, Mary, and Joseph, I love You – Save Souls!!!

St. Michael the Archangel, defend us in battle, be our protection against the wickedness and snares of the devil. Rebuke him O God, we humbly beseech Thee; and do Thou O Prince of the Heavenly host; by the Divine Power thrust into hell satan and all evil spirits, who roam about the world seeking the ruin of souls. Amen.

Mother of Good Counsel

Mary, I renounce my spirit,
and I ask for your spirit.
Mary, take away my thoughts
and give me your thoughts.

BARBARA KLOSS

Mary, take away my desires
and give me your desires.
Mary, take away my feelings
and give me your feelings.

I am totally yours
and everything I have I offer you,
O my beloved Jesus, through
Mary Your Most Holy Mother.

Come Holy Spirit, come by
means of the powerful intercession
of the Immaculate Heart of Mary,
Your well-beloved spouse.

(3 times)
Hail Mary...Mother of Good Counsel,
give us good counsel. Amen.

The Secret Power of the Rosary

"A gold mine of info – jump-start your prayer life!"
Maureen Flynn, editor of Signs and Wonders Magazine

THE SECRET POWER OF THE ROSARY

111 Daily Meditations for Peace and Healing of Families and Nations

BARBARA · KLOSS

any problems in the world start on a spiritual level and manifest in the physical. ⟩ fix them you need the right weapons. The ROSARY is one of the most powerful spiritual weapons!

Maureen Flynn, editor of Signs and Wonders Magazine

sh mystic Barbara Kloss began meditating on the teries of the Rosary per Our lady of Fatima's call. from the beginning, Barbara's First Saturday med- ɔns were dictated by an inward voice which she ·rd and wrote down. In the last five years of her paralyzed by rheumatism, she dictated these itations to a friend or to her nurse. This book is ·esult.

n *The Secret Power of the Rosary:*
ɔgard to the Rosary...the more you know it - the you love it, and the more you love it - the more you ⸜ it.

ɔwer is immense, its action manifold, its domain ·ding, but the vast majority pf people , even those ·love it and say it, do not know its chief and essential ·ing which is the disablement of the demons.

It is necessary by means of the Rosary, to expose this mystery of all their activity in everything. Hence, particularly and universally, is known its efficacious action in:

- healing of the sick
- consoling the sorrowful
- helping the afflicted
- rescue and defense in times of danger
- subduing of evil
- return of sinners
- sanctifying of hearts
- purifying of thoughts
- drawing near to God Himself

$14.95 plus $4.95 S&H

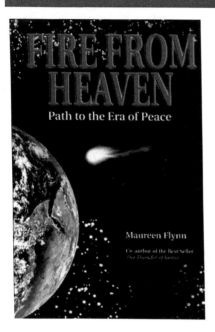

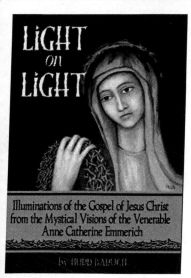
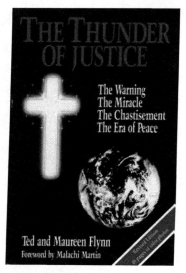

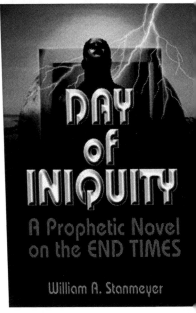

Heaven's Messages for The family

Conversations with Philomena

eaven's Messages for The Family-Vol II
How to become the family God wants
ou to be."The future of humanity passes by
way of the family"
—*Pope John Paul II*

ilies are under attack by the forces of evil, The rise
'vorce, spousal violence and child abuse - all point to
.uation which makes supernatural intervention
ropriate and credible.

Mrs. Janie Garza of Austin, Texas, wife, mother and
tic was chosen by the Lord to be a vessel of simple
holy messages for the family of today. She has been
iving messages and visions since February 15, 1989,
) the present time.

d and Learn about:
hat the main spiritual attacks are against the family
day.

e spiritual tools given by Heaven to combat
e attacks against the family.

nat the roles of the husband, wife and children are
cording to God's divine order.

nat you can do to protect your marriage and family
embers.

e seven visions about the state of the world and
nilies.

. . . .**$14.95 plus $4.95 S&H**

Anchor of Hope from Heaven is a powerful book on messages and revelations from St. Philomena to Janie Garza,
a simple housewife from Texas. This great saint, who is
called **"the wonder-worker"** because of the many miracles occurring through her intercession, is a great saint
for the youth, families and these times.

She is called the **"Anchor of Hope from Heaven"**
to help the families in these troubled times, especially
to help with young children and the youth to help them
to understand that God wants them to remain pure and
holy.

I invite you to welcome St. Philomena into your
families, into your marriages, into your priestly and reli-
gious lives, into your hearts. Trust in her friendship. She
and the blessed Mother, who always accompanies her
daughter, will not disappoint you.
St. Philomena, powerful with God, pray for us!

Read and Learn

- Why is there so much anger and hurt in many young
  people today?
- How does the Evil one use drugs, violence, fornica-
  tion, prostitution, homosexuality , witchcraft, lies,
  profanity and pornography and many other means to
  seduce the youth?
- What powerful weapons can families use to dissolve
  the attacks of Satan?

Dr. Mark Miravalle, S.T. D.
Professor of Theology and Mariology
Franciscan University of Steubenville
. . . .**$14.95 plus $4.95 S&H**

Are You Reading the Signs of the Times?

Signs and Wonders for Our Times Magazine

The awakening hour has come. Our Lord has said that in the midst of great chaos mankind will be awakened. The winds of change are upon the world. The Signs of the Times are multiplying all over the world. Some great events are close at hand...

These disasters are more than isolated events. Today, Heaven is issuing extraordinary warnings to the world — warnings you hear when you read Signs and Wonders for Our Times

- Medjugorje. Betania, Venezuela, Garabandal, Spain... Heaven speaks to the world
- Earthquakes, Tsunamis, and terrorism—signs of tribulation
- What sin is bringing judgement on our world?
- One world Government is here...!
- Loss of Faith: What the Bible says about the Great Apostasy.
- Recent Hurricane Season, worst on record—Katrina was deadliest and most costly catastrophe in U.S. Histroy.

Read Signs and Wonders for Our Times and discover we are living in critical times. But you'll also discover how to respond to Heaven's warnings and messages!

Yes I wish to send a year's gift subscription of *Signs and Wonders for Our Times* to the person(s) indicated below. Please send me my free gift od Divine Mercy prayer card.

Name _____

Address _____

City _____ State _____ Zip _____

Phone: (H) _____ (W) _____

My first gift subscription—$35.00   Name _____

Address _____

City/State/Zip _____

*$35 U.S.   **$48 Canada**   **and $70 Foreign**

Method of Payment

☐ I have enclosed my check   ☐☐☐ 3 digit VIN code

☐ Visa or MasterCard Number (circle one)_____ Expiration Date _____

Signature _____ Phone Number _____

You may order from Signs and Wonders for Our Times by mail, phone, or fax

Mail your orders to Signs and Wonders for Our Times, P.O. Box 345, Herndon, VA 20172-0345
Phone your order to 703 707 0799. Fax orders to 703 707 0557

Order online at www.sign.org